BEST
ONE-ACT PLAYS

BEST
ONE-ACT PLAYS

Los Angeles Actors' Theatre / Los Angeles Theatre Center

edited by Joseph Scott Kierland

PANJANDRUM BOOKS, INC.
Los Angeles • 1985

Copyright © 1985 by Panjandrum Books. All rights reserved. No part of this book may be reprinted or reproduced in any form, except for brief excerpts which are part of a review, without permission in writing from the publisher.

First Printing.

Library of Congress Cataloging in Publication Data
Main entry under title:

Best one-act plays from LAAT/Los Angeles Theatre Center.

   Contents: Tom & Jerry / Jim Geoghan—Triplet / Kitty Johnson—Junk food / Willard Manus — [etc.]
   1. One-act plays, American   2. American drama—20th century.   I. Kierland, Joseph Scott, 1932–
II. Los Angeles Theatre Center.
PS627.O53B4   1984   812'.041'08   84-25433
ISBN 0-915572-79-6
ISBN 0-915572-78-8 (pbk.)

The following plays were previously copyrighted by the authors:

Tom & Jerry copyright © 1983 by Jim Geoghan.

Triplet copyright © 1981 by Kitty Johnson. *Strawberry Envy* copyright © 1983 by Kitty Johnson.

Junk Food copyright © 1982 by Willard Manus.

On a Cold and Frosty Morning copyright © 1960 by Joseph Scott Kierland.

Brutal Mandate copyright © 1982 by Craig Pettigrew.

They Won't Let Me Pay Your Rent, Jack! copyright © 1970 by Alan Ormsby.

Prowlers copyright © 1980 by Paul Minx.

The Meeting copyright © 1984 by Jeffrey Stetson.

Cover photo: Jeff Peters
Cover design: Cindy Cancio, Manna Graphics (Los Angeles), and Joseph Scott Kierland.

Manufactured in the United States of America.

This book was funded in part by a grant from the The National Endowment for the Arts, Literature Program, a federal agency.

Panjandrum Books, 11321 Iowa Ave., Suite 1, Los Angeles, CA 90025

For RALPH WAITE *who lit the fire,*
and to
BILL BUSHNELL *who keeps it burning.*

CONTENTS

Preface
Joseph Scott Kierland vii

Plays
TOM & JERRY
  Jim Geoghan 1
TRIPLET
  Kitty Johnson 20
JUNK FOOD
  Willard Manus 36
ON A COLD AND FROSTY MORNING
  Joseph Scott Kierland 56
BRUTAL MANDATE
  Craig Pettigrew 67
THEY WON'T LET ME
PAY YOUR RENT, JACK!
  Alan Ormsby 86
PROWLERS
  Paul Minx 99
STRAWBERRY ENVY
  Kitty Johnson 114
THE MEETING
  Jeff Stetson 132
About LAAT/Los Angeles Theater Center 157
About the Playwrights 158
About the Producers 159

PREFACE

WE ARE A SOCIETY OF ONE-ACT WATCHERS

The One-Act play is our oldest and most enduring dramatic form with its roots in the Classic Greek tragedies and comedies. Aeschylus, Sophocles, Euripides and Aristophanes wrote One-Acts, and the Western World has continued to watch them throughout the theatre's twenty-five-hundred-year history. Even today, literally millions of people stare at Situation Comedies, Soap-Operas, and Re-Runs in an endless wheel of One-Acts. We are a society of One-Act watchers because there are certain advantages to watching them.

One-Acts are short, concise and should have all the elements of a Full-Length play without forcing the audience to sit for a very long time. One-Acts are much more convenient, and with the advent of television we have devised a way to get our daily dose of One-Acts without even having to leave our living rooms.

Ahhh, but in those twenty-five centuries from Aeschylus to Norman Lear, something has been lost. The One-Act Play's slide into television has left us very little *except* the convenience of sitting in our living room. Oedipus, Agamemnon and Electra no longer haunt our world. Now it is Archie Bunker, Laverne and Shirley, and J. R. Ewing. What happened?

Simply, the One-Act was drained from the theatre and poured into radio, and then into television. With each step, it became more caricatured and took on the dimensions of the Comic Strip. The only thing the television Sitcom and the Soap-Opera did *not* take from the Comic Strip were the balloons with the words in them. Or to be more precise, the television One-Act is simply a short piece of dramatic narrative that is constantly being interrupted by other little dramatic devices called 'commercials.' Added to its problems, the television One-Act has extremely tight time restrictions, demands for 'running-characterizations,' and its primary function is to keep you in your seat so that those little commercials can sell their wonderful products to your entire family. It is difficult to overcome restrictions like these, and the end result is that television One-Acts at their dramatic and comedic best are total mediocrity.

So what has happened to our twenty-five hundred year tradition of One-Acts? Has television destroyed them with its mindless prattle and its constant commercial interruptions? No—the One-Act continues to be alive and well in our theatres, and particularly at the Los Angeles Actors' Theatre (now called the Los Angeles Theatre Center).

In this first collection of LAAT plays, we have nine of the finest One-Acts from their annual Festival of World Premieres. Included in this first volume is a wide variety of theatrical styles, ranging from the comedic realism of *TOM & JERRY* and the cutting surrealistic edge of *THEY WON'T LET ME PAY YOUR RENT, JACK!* to the horrifying absurdity in *ON A COLD AND FROSTY MORNING*. There is also an American political tragedy depicted in *BRUTAL MANDATE*, and our society's paranoid fears and entrapments are wrestled to laughter in *PROWLERS* and *JUNK FOOD*. And Kitty Johnson's *TRIPLET* and *STRAWBERRY ENVY* truly show one of the most unique and personal playwrighting styles in theatre today. And finally, THE MEETING brings together the two great black leaders, Dr. Martin Luther King, Jr. and Malcolm X just before their inevitable assassinations.

The remarkable thing about these plays is that they have all been written and developed at the Playwrights' Lab of the Los Angeles Actors' Theatre. The LAAT gives its space, its time, and its encouragement so that its playwrights can write without any restrictions on their style, time or subject matter. In this way, the LAAT's audiences are constantly being surprised, challenged and entertained by a daring, modern theatre that has a total freedom of expression.

These nine plays are just a few from the wide variety that a prolific theatre, like the LAAT, has to offer. And after twenty-five hundred years, the One-Act play continues to be as young as ever.

Joseph Scott Kierland

TOM & JERRY
(Louis B. Mayer Award Winner)

(from the collection, ONLY KIDDING)
by
JIM GEOGHAN

(The play was first presented at the Los Angeles Actors' Theatre's Louis B. Mayer Playwrights' Festival in 1983.)

Original Cast
(In Order of Appearance)

JERRY GOLDSTEIN	Mark Goldstein
TOM KELLY	Greg Monaghan
SAL D'ANGELO	Sam Zap

Directed by .... Phil Boroff
Produced by .... Adam Leipzig & Diane White

Bill Bushnell, Artistic Producing Director

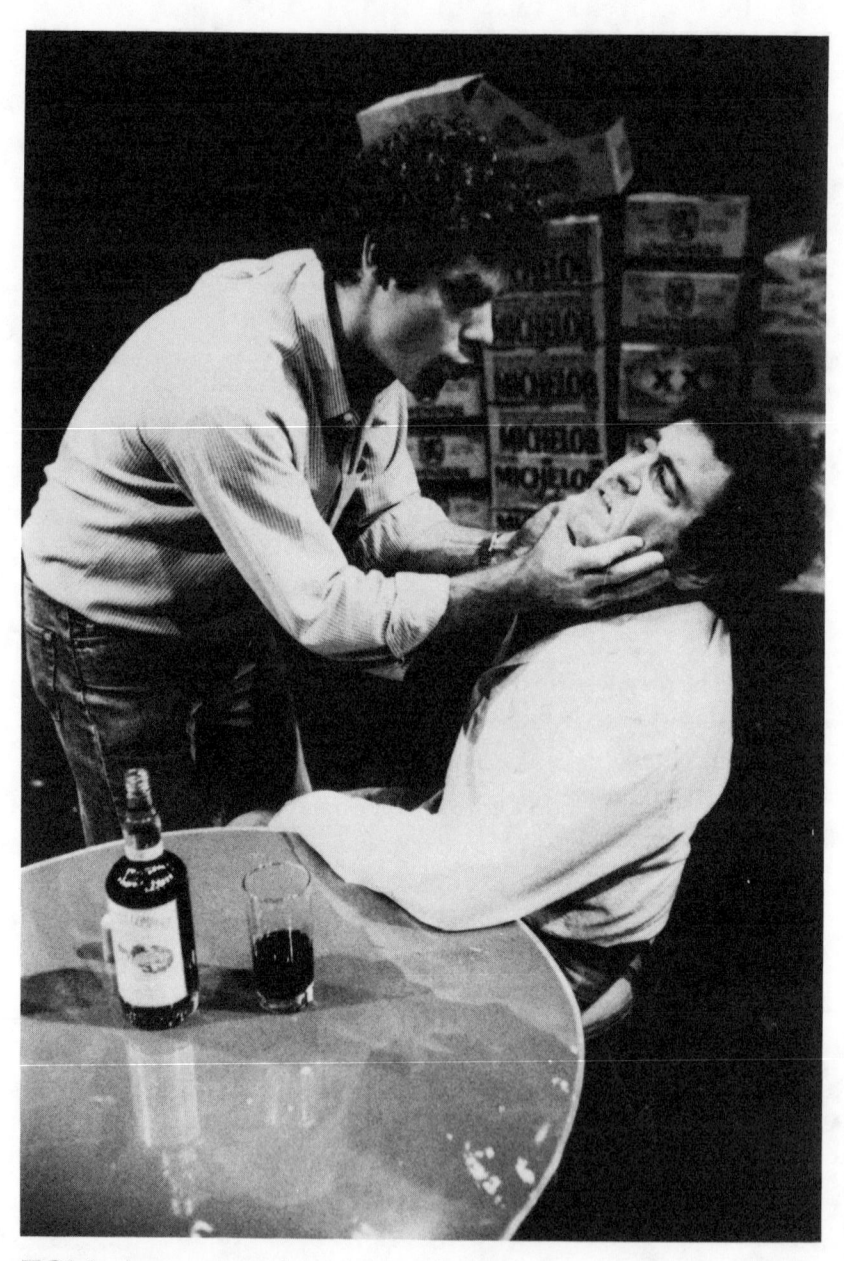

TOM: Are you in there somewhere?!!

[*Lights up on a niteclub basement. The room is nothing more than a cold, dark cellar that serves as a dressing room for the performers who appear at the niteclub. It is stacked with cases of liquor, beer, wine and soda. There is a collection of dusty, broken chairs and tables stacked high in one corner. Various articles one might find in a niteclub (glassware, candles, swizzle sticks, etc.) lie about. In the background lie old advertising posters for the niteclub reading "Disco Dance Contest," "Mon. Night-Foxy Boxing." Downstage center are three chairs and a table looking as dusty and broken as the others stacked in the background. A payphone is mounted on the wall stage right. Stage left is a doorway leading to the niteclub. There is also a doorway leading to a bathroom. We hear audience applause and whistles from offstage as* TOM *and* JERRY *enter.* JERRY *carries a cassette tape recorder in one hand, a glass of cola in the other. They are all keyed up and excited having done a good show at the club. The applause and whistles slowly fade off.*]

TOM: Good show.
JERRY: Good? It was terrific!
TOM: You see the guy in the front row? How hard he laughed?
JERRY: The fat guy?
TOM: Yeah, him.
JERRY: He laughed so hard he almost dropped his gun.

[JERRY *has put down his glass of cola and tape recorder. The two continue to talk as* JERRY *crosses to the payphone, inserts coins and dials.*]

TOM: You messed up, though.
JERRY: What do you mean I messed up?
TOM: You dropped some lines. A whole section.
JERRY: Hey, we're a *team*, remember? We don't mess up individually.
 If something goes wrong it's because of *us*. Together.
TOM: Okay, so "we" messed up tonight.
JERRY: That's it.
TOM: Because *you* dropped some lines.
JERRY: Cute. [*into phone like a stereotypical homosexual*] Yes, this is
 Jerry Goldstein.
TOM: What are you doing?
JERRY: [*Sotto to* TOM *as himself.*] Calling my answering service. You talk
 like a fag and they don't put you on hold. [*Into phone gay again:*]
 Hmm? She did? When did that come in? [*Pause.*] Oh, goodie gumdrops. Ciao.

[JERRY *hangs up the phone and crosses to the table where he has his appointment book. He searches for a phone number.*]

TOM: Did we get the whole show on the machine?
JERRY: We sure did. Listen.

[JERRY *presses the "play" button and we hear the same audience applause and whistles. As it plays.*]

TOM: That's not the part I want to hear.

JERRY: It's the part *I* want to hear.

TOM: I want to go back to the beginning. Where "we" messed up.

JERRY: [*Shutting off machine.*] What for?

TOM: Jerry, do you realize we haven't done a new bit in over eight months?

JERRY: Bullshit. We do new stuff all the time.

TOM: Bits and pieces. A line here, a line there. Hunks. Hunks. I want to do new hunks.

JERRY: Why's it so important?

TOM: Because I am bored to shit with our old stuff. I'm daydreaming on stage. Right in the middle of bits I'm saying the words, I'm making the moves but my mind is wondering if the blonde waitress has got big sloppy nipples or teeny-tiny ones.

JERRY: [*Praying.*] Oh, please let them be big and sloppy.

TOM: We had a hunk to do tonight. We wrote in on the Belt Parkway. We rehearsed it on the Brooklyn/Queens Expressway. We forgot to do it on stage. I want to listen to the tape and find out why.

JERRY: Later. I've got to do this now. I got a message from my agent.

[JERRY *crosses to the payphone, inserts coins and dials.*]

TOM: It's ten-thirty. She's not in her office now.

JERRY: I'm calling her at home. The two best kept secrets in New York are my agent's home phone number and the combination to her chastity belt.

TOM: I'll bet.

JERRY: Funny thing is . . . one's worth a fortune. The other's not worth shit. [*Into phone ultra sweet and phony.*] Barbara? Jer here. I got your message. Am I calling too late? Hmm? Am I? [*Pause.*] Aha ha ha ha ha ha!!!

[JERRY *laughs too loud and too long.* TOM *silently mimics* JERRY's *phony laugh behind his back.*]

What are you doing? Hum? Something dirty? Hmm? [*Pause.*] Aha ha ha ha!!!

[*Again* JERRY *laughs too loud and too long.* TOM *mimics the phony laugh again.*]

I *did*? I *got* it? The commercial? Really? The Yippie National? Oh, marvey! Simply, absolutely marvey!

[TOM *silently mouths the word "marvey" in disbelief.*]

I'm not surprised. The director said I was the only actor who auditioned who could give him exactly what he wanted.

[TOM *mimes a blowjob behind* JERRY's *back.*]

You're a doll, you know that? A complete and absolute doll. [*Pause.*] Yes, I'll talk with you in the morning. Now you go back to what you were doing, okay? But be careful. You'll go blind. Aha ha ha ha!!! [*Hangs up phone.*] Chee! What a cold ass bitch she is!
TOM: Who? Barbara? Your commercial agent?
JERRY: Real mean, cold ass bitch.
TOM: But you sounded so lovey-dovey with her on the phone.
JERRY: Eyuck! She makes me wanna *puke!*
TOM: Must be a lot of work in the morning.
JERRY: What.
TOM: Shaving two faces.
JERRY: Cute. Very cute.
TOM: You got another commercial?
JERRY: Yeah. Yippie dogfood. It's a national, too. I film it next week. Guess who the director is.
TOM: No idea.
JERRY: Sam Peckinpaw.
TOM: Yeah, sure.
JERRY: This dog won't eat Yippie dogfood.
TOM: Right.
JERRY: So I shoot 'im.
TOM: Kids oughta love it.

[TOM *takes a drink from* JERRY's *glass of cola and gasps from the strong alcohol content. He gasps for air.*]

Cough! Woa . . . what the . . . what *is* this?
JERRY: A little something to keep the cords oiled.
TOM: You were drinking this? On stage?
JERRY: Yeah, my voice was a little tight.
TOM: This is not for drinking.
JERRY: It's not?
TOM: It's for stripping wax off of kitchen floors.
JERRY: C'mon, it's just a little rum and Coke.
TOM: [*Imitating electronic penalty buzzer.*] Ehhh! Wrong, can you take it Purdue? This is a *lot* of rum . . . very little Coke.
JERRY: Aw, get off my back.
TOM: You never did that before. Drink on stage. During a show.
JERRY: Yeah, well I also never had five commercial auditions in one day. That's how many I had today. Five auditions. My voice was almost shot.

TOM: Aw, what horseshit!
JERRY: Each audition was worse than the one before. I'm sitting in some casting director's outer office, trying to learn my commercial copy and who walks in but some *face*.
TOM: Face?
JERRY: Face! Some face I've seen eighteen billion times on TV doing this commercial, that commercial. Cool, confident, ready to score another commercial. Then there's another face. And another.
TOM: Wait a minute. Who are these guys?
JERRY: That's just it. I don't know. They're good. Real good. They work all the time. They get commercials one after the other. And I'm reading for the same part. The pressure is incredible, man. You have no idea.
TOM: [*Indicates glass.*] So you have to drink *that* on stage to loosen up?!
JERRY: I already told you! It's for my chords. My voice was shot.
TOM: That's why you forgot the new lines tonight. Isn't it!
JERRY: I said *back off*!!! Jeez . . . guy has a little drink you gotta make it sound like mass murder. C'mon, Kelly. Lighten up. We did a good show tonight. Now it's time to cruise the bar for chicks. Bring them down here into our deluxe dressing room.
TOM: Yeah, sure.
JERRY: Let them perform oral sex upon our organs.
TOM: Aw, don't start that again.
JERRY: Hey, you never know, man. You never know.
TOM: Jerry, how long have you been a comedian?
JERRY: As long as we've been together. Five years.
TOM: And in those five years how many times have you gotten laid as a direct result of your being a comedian?
JERRY: As a *direct* result?
TOM: Direct, indirect, whatever.
JERRY: [*Thinks, then.*] None.
TOM: I keep telling you: bass players and drummers . . . *they* get blowjobs in their dressing room.
JERRY: And what do comedy teams get?
TOM: Hah. Comedy teams . . . If we're lucky we get to sniff the sofa.
JERRY: Still there's hope. Hope that out there in this world there's a young and beautiful girl with a very low I.Q. and equally low self-esteem . . . looking to get back at her parents in her own peculiar way . . . by having sex with complete strangers . . . who don't care about her.
TOM: That's a beautiful dream, Jer.
JERRY: I know. I'm a hopeless romantic.
TOM: Hold on to that dream. Hold on to it.
JERRY: Yeah, I'll hold on to the dream. I just want to find some chick to

hold on to *this*. [*Grabs crotch.*] Known in Latin American countries as "El Jackhammero".
TOM: El *what*?
JERRY: It's a new name I came up with for my peenie. Like it? It was a tossup between that and "The Punisher". "El Jackhammero" won for it's foreign flair.
TOM: You want "foreign flair" why don't you call it what it really is. "El Tacquito"! I've seen you naked at the health club, my man. You've got some nerve calling it that.
JERRY: Aw, there you go spoiling everything for me again. What are you happy now?
TOM: Is that what you do all day? When you're not out on commercial calls? Think up names for your *dick*?
JERRY: I know it doesn't sound like an elegant pastime but it gives me something to do.

[JERRY *has helped himself to a bottle of Southern Comfort from one of the boxes.* HE *opens the bottle and gestures at* TOM.]

Wanna hit?
TOM: No thanks.
JERRY: You call yourself Irish?
TOM: I'm fighting the stereotype.
JERRY: [*Taking a swig.*] So am I.

[JERRY *drinks hard and often throughout. He reaches into a pocket and takes out some pills.*]

Want one?
TOM: What are they?
JERRY: White Crosses. They make the brain sharp. You could use some.
TOM: Where'd you get those?
JERRY: From Sal.

[TOM *reacts.*]

C'mon, don't look so surprised. You think he drives a Porsche like the one he's got from selling beer and Seven-Ups?

[JERRY *takes some pills and washes them down with a slug from the bottle.*]

TOM: Phew . . . White Crosses and Southern Comfort . . .
JERRY: Yeah, the cocktail o' rock stars.
TOM: You're crazy, man! You know that!
JERRY: Think I'll stay up all night tonight.
TOM: After those pills you've got no choice.
JERRY: I've got a nine AM audition tomorrow. Might as well stay up. Couldn't sleep if I wanted to.

TOM: Why do you bother with it, Jerry?
JERRY: Why? For the *money* is why. It's going to help me overcome the three things I've got going against me in life.
TOM: Uh uh . . . not again.

[JERRY *becomes enthused. He wants* TOM *to play along and do a routine they've obviously done before.*]

JERRY: C'mon, do it, Tommy.
TOM: No way.
JERRY: Come on!
TOM: No.
JERRY: Please? Pretty please, milk an' honey on it?
TOM: Okay, just this once but you've got to promise me never to drink again during a show. Promise?
JERRY: [*Crossing fingers behind his back.*] Swear to God.

[TOM *and* JERRY *quickly take on performing aires.*]

TOM: In the beginning God decided to make some people poor . . .
JERRY: [*Pathetic, poor character.*] Got a nickel?
TOM: . . . some people ugly . . .
JERRY: [*Contorting his face.*] Eeeeeeyuck!!!
TOM: . . . and some people Jewish.
JERRY: Oy-*vay*!
TOM: But He made Jerry Goldstein all *three*.
JERRY: Tah dah! [*to* TOM] But I'm doin' commercials now, God and I make a lotta money.
TOM: [*Deep, God-like voice.*] Good boy, Jerald.
JERRY: And some day I'll get on the "Buddy King Show" and no one who gets on network TV is ugly.
TOM: Beauty by association. Invented it myself.
JERRY: And when I become successful . . . a show biz institution . . .
TOM: Yes?
JERRY: I can deny ever being Jewish again.
TOM: And some day young Jerald will overcome this triple threat, this dreaded disease for which there is no known cure. . . .
JERRY: Hope so.
TOM: And become rich, handsome and gentile. To live his sunset years with a pipe and elbow patches as Leave It To Beaver's father . . . Ward Cleaver.
JERRY: [*Mimes pipe, a la Ward Cleaver calling.*] "June, I'm home. Wally? Beaver?"

[TOM *and* JERRY *chuckle a bit over the fun they've had with each other.*]

TOM: Funny . . .

JERRY: You know what? We're too damn good for toilets like this. Look at this dump. And we're working for chump change.
TOM: Yeah, but I take that chump change and pay my chump landlord with it.
JERRY: I've been thinking. We ought to cut this dump loose. Work the showcase clubs in the city. That's where all the big agents go.
TOM: But you *have* an agent.
JERRY: I might want a *better* one. And they're not out here in Brooklyn.
TOM: But the *money* is here.
JERRY: The money here is crap.
TOM: True. But the money at the showcase clubs is *less* than crap.
JERRY: Aw!
TOM: Five bucks and a free drink. I can't live on that.
JERRY: What are you worried for? You're still writing gags for whatsisface, aren't you?
TOM: Steven MacLain?
JERRY: Yeah, him. That no talent, polyester scum wad who goes on talk shows and talks about his fuckin' *feet*! Like we really wanna know, right?
TOM: Sure, I write some gags but it . . .
JERRY: [*Interrupts.*] How could you do that, anyway? I mean write for some guy like that?
TOM: Well, artistically speaking I know it doesn't rank up there with Yippie dogfood commercials.
JERRY: I just think we're better than toilets like this. And Sal . . . he treats stupidity like it's some kind of career goal. Tommy, I swear, if his I.Q. was one point lower he'd be a crustacean.
TOM: Sal's been good to us, Jer. He pays on time and in cash.

[SAL *enters holding a bottle of champagne and stands there listening.* JERRY *doesn't see* SAL *yet. Neither does* TOM.]

JERRY: He's a dumb, stupid, ignorant asshole who doesn't pay us *half* of what we're worth. . . .

[TOM *sees* SAL *standing there and warns* JERRY.]

TOM: Ahem.
JERRY: [*Instantly catches on, covering.*] . . . and I don't ever wanna see that guy in Boston ever again. And that's that!
TOM: Hey, Sal!

[JERRY *swings around and pretends to be surprised to see* SAL.]

JERRY: Sal! Baby! [*To* TOM.] C'mon, Tommy. Let's get 'im.

[TOM *and* JERRY *rush over to* SAL. TOM *stands behind* SAL *holding his arms as* JERRY *gives* SAL *the third degree. This is obviously a game they play often and* SAL *loves it.*]

TOM: Had the nerve to show up, eh?
JERRY: Okay, Sal . . . where's our dough?
SAL: [*Playing along.*] I ain't got it.
JERRY: Ya hear that, Noodles? He says he ain't got it.
TOM: He's lyin'!
JERRY: C'mon, fish face. Where's the dough?
SAL: I swear I ain't got it.
JERRY: Listen up, you piece o' spit. We can do this the hard way . . . or we can do it the hard way. It's up to you.
SAL: Oh my God . . . please don't hurt me. . . .
TOM: Break his legs, Jer.

[JERRY *digs through* SAL's *pockets and withdraws some money.*]

JERRY: So! Ya ain't got it, eh?
TOM: He was holdin' out on us!

[JERRY *slaps* SAL *in the face with the money.*]

JERRY: We don't like guys what hold out on us, ya unnerstand?
SAL: I swear. I don't know how that money got there.
JERRY: You asked for it, ya piece o' spit.

[TOM *lets go of* SAL. *The two stand before* SAL *and run an assortment of Three Stooges noises and gestures at him.*]

TOM & JERRY: Wu wu wu wu wu wu!!! Na na na na na!!! La dee dah!!! Ruff!!! Ruff!!!

[SAL *is reduced to a helpless puddle of laughter.*]

SAL: Aw, shit . . . Oh! That's funny! You guys is demented, you know that? You're demented.
JERRY: Thank you.

[JERRY *counts the money and gives* TOM *his half.*]

SAL: You did a real good show tonight. We're very pleased.
TOM: Thanks.
SAL: I swear, I can watch you guys do them bits over an' over an' over. . .
TOM: You do. Every week.
SAL: I even know some of your stuff by heart, I swear.
JERRY: Yeah?
SAL: Yeah. I could repeat some of your bits *every single word*.
TOM: Wish I could say the same about Jerry.
SAL: Every time you come out here I see them same bits, I figure I'll get tired of 'em but I don't!

JERRY: Uh . . . we were going to do some new bits tonight but uh . . . Tom forgot.
SAL: Really? How's it go?
JERRY: Well, remember when you were a kid . . . the way kids used to insult each other's mother?
TOM: Like your mother's so low she could play handball against a curb.
SAL: Right, right.
JERRY: Or your mother's like a police station. Dicks are comin' in and out all the time.
SAL: Yeah, sure. I remember. Or like uh . . . [*Trying to remember.*] hold it . . . uh . . . ya mother eats shit!

[TOM *and* JERRY *react. There is a pregnant silence. Finally:*]

JERRY: Something like that.
TOM: Anyway, do you think kids in other countries do the same thing?
SAL: I dunno.
TOM: Two kids in England insulting each other's mother. Right? Two English kids.

[TOM *and* JERRY *assume the mannerisms of two ultra-cultured and prissy upper-class English children.*]

TOM: I say!
JERRY: Yes?
TOM: Your mother is . . . inappropriate.
JERRY: How dare you. You take that back.
TOM: I shan't
JERRY: You shat.
TOM: I shan't
JERRY: You shat. Because *your* mother . . .
TOM: Yes?
JERRY: Your mother is . . . ostentatious.
TOM: You despicable lout!
JERRY: Watch your mouth, dear boy.
TOM: You're dashing for a thrashing.
SAL: Aw, shit! That's funny!
TOM: [*As himself.*] Okay. Two Polish kids doing the same thing.
JERRY: Two kids in Poland.

[TOM *and* JERRY *muss their hair, pull their shirttails out, whatever makes them look "stupid". They almost scream at each other in thick Polish accents.*]

TOM: Hey, you person!
JERRY: What? Me?
TOM: Your mother . . . she is sleeping withs . . . your *father!!!*
JERRY: Nooooo!!!

TOM: YES!!!
JERRY: Your mother then . . . she is *good cook*!!!
TOM: NOOOO!!!
JERRY: Aha ha ha!!!
TOM: Your mother . . . *pretty*!!!
JERRY: I hate you!!!
SAL: [*Laughing.*] Aw, shit! That's funny! I love you fuckin' guys, you know that?
JERRY: Oh . . . you love us enough to bring your silver bullet?
SAL: Right here.

[SAL *reaches into his pocket and hands* JERRY *a cocaine bullet.* JERRY *takes a huge hit up each nostril.*]

JERRY: Knnn! Alright! Knnn! Jeez!

[JERRY *hands the bullet back to* SAL.]

SAL: [*To* TOM.] Wanna hit?
TOM: No thanks. I'm driving our spacecraft back to the city.

[JERRY *struts about feeling terrific from the hit.*]

JERRY: Mmm, yeah. Man, I feel *good*.
TOM: Must be those whole grain breads at breakfast.
JERRY: [*Registers bottle.*] Champagne? Special occasion, Sal?
SAL: Guess you might say that.
JERRY:[*Lifts bottle to examine.*] Expensive stuff. What is it? Jimmy Hoffa's birthday?
SAL: Naw, nothin' like that.
TOM: You look like you know a secret, Sal.
SAL: Guess I do. An' it's a biggie.
JERRY: Well, give! Give!
SAL: Okay, but gimme time. I wanna tell this thing in my own way, ya know?
JERRY: Your way can take *months*.
SAL: Well, it's the only way I know. I got some news for yas.
TOM: Good news?
SAL: Could be. You remember a couple of weeks ago I had my cousin Carmine come down here with his videotape shit and make a cassette thing of you guys?
JERRY: Sal, you ever think about teaching linguistics at Harvard?
SAL: Huh?
TOM: Jerry . . .!
JERRY: Sorry. Go ahead.
SAL: You remember. I told you guys it was for Carmine. The tape thing. You know, he likes comedians and likes to make tapes and shit.
TOM: Yeah.

SAL: Well, that was sorta like a lie. I didn't wanna get ya hopes up or nothin' but the tape wasn't for Carmine.
JERRY: Who was it for?
SAL: Well, I got some friends who know some people and them people . . . they know Buddy King.
TOM: Buddy King?
JERRY: *The* Buddy King?
SAL: I sent the tape to Buddy King. Through my friends. He's always lookin' for funny, young comedians for his show, right?
TOM: And?
SAL: And he fuckin' *loved* you guys. He saw the tape. He wants yas to do his show.
JERRY: He . . .h . . .
TOM: He *what!*
SAL: Buddy King says you can do his show any time you guys want!
TOM: My God. . . .
JERRY: Oho! Oh! Oh my God!!!

[JERRY *paces the floor in wild excitement, jumping up and down, throwing punches with his fist.* TOM *is ecstatic, too, but much less animated.*]

My God!!! Holey SHIT!!! Yeah!!! The Buddy King Show!!! I don't believe it!!!
SAL: You guys don't have to say yes or no right away.
JERRY: Buddy Fuckin' King!!!
SAL: You can take time to think it over.
JERRY: Hah!!! Yeah!!! Ho boy!!!
SAL: [*To* TOM.] What's he doin'?
TOM: That's Jerry "thinking it over".

[JERRY *crosses to the champagne bottle, pops the cork, gives the bottle a shake and sprays everyone and everything in sight. He finishes up pouring the champagne over his head.*]

JERRY: Holey shit!!! This is terrific!!! The Buddy King Show!!! Who-EEE!!!
TOM: Jerry! Watch it!
SAL: Eh, careful. You'll get the contract wet.
TOM: What contract?
SAL: I thought it would be good if we put some stuff in writing sorta.
TOM: What kind of stuff?
SAL: To be honest with ya I wanna manage you guys. Help your careers. Be there for things ya need. [*withdraws contract*] It's just a standard kinda management contract here. Just . . . standard. [*withdraws pens*] Got a fifty dollar Parker Pen for yas. Got one for each of yas. You can keep the pens.
JERRY: [*Grabbing pen.*] Terrific. Where do we sign.

SAL: On the last page where it says . . .
TOM: [*Snatching contract.*] Maybe we should *read* it first? Huh, Jerry?
JERRY: What's to read? We're going to be on the Buddy King Show! Oh, baby! I can't believe it.
TOM: Is this like a package deal, Sal?
SAL: Huh?
TOM: I mean if we don't sign the contract do we still get to do the Buddy King Show?
SAL: Boy, you really put me on the spot there, Tommy.
JERRY: Tom, what are you putting Sal on the spot for, huh?
TOM: I just want to know, that's all.
SAL: There's a lot of interest up at the Buddy King Show over you guys. But that interest has come from me. Ya understand that? Comes time for them to send a contract . . . I'm not your manager. . . .I'm out of a deal. I'm gonna look real stupid to them. I got a reputation to protect. They'll say "Eh, Sal . . . are we dealin' with you or no?" I'll have to say "No". I'm gonna look like a real asshole. I don't know if I can keep the deal alive if I'm not in on it.
JERRY: So we'll sign! We'll sign!
TOM: Jerry, don't you want to see what we're getting into?
JERRY: We're getting "into" the Buddy King Show! That's all I need to know. Five years we've been trying to get on that show. Five *years*! Didn't I tell you I felt good tonight? Didn't I? You feel good . . . good things happen. You *make* them happen. You draw them *to* you. Like Sal. My pizanne!

[JERRY *hugs* SAL *and helps himself to his silver bullet. He snorts up both nostrils.*]

Knnn! Yeah! Damn I feel *good*! Feelin' even better! Knnn!

[JERRY *tosses the bullet back to* SAL.]
TOM: If you were our manager we'd still need a booking agent, wouldn't we?
SAL: Got some lined up. No problem gettin' you guys with someone.
TOM: So we'd pay our commission to you. . . . [*looking through contract*] What is it . . . ten percent? Fifteen?
SAL: Thirty.
JERRY: And he's worth every penny of it.
SAL: I'll be losin' money the first three years, believe me.
TOM: Thirty percent to you, another ten to the agent . . . it means we'd each be working for thirty cents on the dollar.
SAL: If you wanna look at it *that* way.
JERRY: [*Singing in a world of his own.*] "Here's Buddy, my buddy . . . our buddy boy. . . ."
SAL: There's a lotta work we could pick up for you guys. Vegas, Reno, Atlantic City . . . Miami.

JERRY: Miami! I can visit my grandmother!
TOM: Would we be working the main rooms?
SAL: Not right away. Mostly lounges to start.
JERRY: [*Singing.*] "When you need a friend, who's the living end, who could do most anything . . ."
TOM: Jerry, I'm trying to talk over here.
JERRY: [*Singing right at Tom.*] "Call Buddy . . . your buddy . . . here's Buddy King!!!"

[JERRY *suddenly realizes he's about to throw up.*]

Oh . . . shit. . . .

[JERRY *dashes off into the bathroom. We hear him throwing up offstage.*]

ARRRRRRRF!!!
SAL: There goes four hundred bucks right into the toilet.
TOM: So, we would work the lounges, huh?
SAL: Yeah, opening for singers, guys like that. The people I know got a whole bunch of singers you could open for. Joey Vee . . . ever hear of him?
TOM: No.
SAL: You will. He's the next Vic Damone, believe me. Tommy Ventura. You musta heard of him.
TOM: No.
JERRY: [*Offstage.*] ARRRRRRF!!!
SAL: He's terrific. He's the next Beatles. There's a lotta guys you could work with. A lotta guys.
TOM: And no contract . . . no "Buddy King Show . . . ?"
SAL: C'mon, you're not a baby. They call it "show *business*" not "show *friendship*". It's just a standard contract, Tommy. You know, I get some singers in here, some rock and roll groups . . . they've heard I'm lookin' to get into management and stuff. They go "Eh, Sal! Why don't you manage *us*?" And I go "Maybe in another lifetime . . ." Because they all got one thing in common.
TOM: What's that?
SAL: They're stupid. All the singers and shit . . . they're stupid is what they are. The people I know, my friends, my bartenders, my waitresses . . . don't get me wrong . . . they're all nice people . . . but they're stupid, too. Everyone I know is stupid. Everyone who works here wears the same clothes, drives the same fuckin' Trans Am . . . nobody ever says anything that's clever, stuff like that. The most clever thing anyone ever says around here is "fuckin' A". That's it. Sometimes I think I'm gonna drown in stupid people. Sometimes I think I'm kinda stupid myself.
TOM: Aw, Sal . . . c'mon.

SAL: Naw, that's alright. I know I'm not that smart. But you guys . . . I watch yas talk, perform on stage . . . you make up jokes left and right . . . you're so clever and shit I can't believe what I'm seein' sometimes. I get angry inside. I tell myself "How come you can't make up shit like that!" In my circle of friends guys like you . . .
TOM: Yeah?
SAL: You're from another *planet*. I don't wanna do what everybody else here does. There's something inside me that's very restless. You know what I'm talking about? You know that feeling?
TOM: Yeah.
SAL: I knew you would. I wanna manage a comedy team. The best comedy team there is in the world. You guys. I would work very hard for you, Tommy. Try and think what your lives would be like if I could manage you guys.
JERRY: [*Offstage.*] ARRRRRF!!!
SAL: Think it over.

[SAL *exits. After a few beats* JERRY *enters from the bathroom wiping his hands on a paper towel.*]

JERRY: Where's Sal?
TOM: He just left. How do you feel?
JERRY: Terrific! I swear, I never felt better in my whole life. Where's the contract? You didn't give it back to Sal, did you?
TOM: No, it's right here.
JERRY: [*Takes pen and readies to sign.*] Good, good . . . I didn't sign it yet.
TOM: Jerry . . .
JERRY: [*Looking at contract.*] You didn't sign it either.
TOM: I know. I thought we should talk about it first.
JERRY: What's to talk about? We're going to do the "Buddy King Show." Oh, man! We're gonna be rich, you know that? RICH! Tommy, I'm gonna buy you your own white woman.
TOM: Jerry. . . .
JERRY: Uh uh uh uh uh . . . I insist.
TOM: Jerry!
JERRY: Yeah?
TOM: I think signing a management contract with Sal could be the worst mistake of our entire lives.
JERRY: I think it's the best thing that ever happened to us.
TOM: Well, at least we don't disagree by much.
JERRY: Tom, Sal's got us our shot. All we have to do is sign.
TOM: All we have to do is *not* sign . . . keep doing good shows, get better and better as an act. We'll get on the Buddy King Show *without* getting involved with Sal.

JERRY: Aw, Sal's a pussycat. So what if he's a little mobbed up?
TOM: A "little mobbed up!" He named his first-born daughter Jimmy the Weasel! It's not worth it, Jerry. You should see this contract. It's for seven years. Seven *years*, Jerry.
JERRY: Seven's my lucky number.
TOM: Sal wants thirty percent *before* an agent takes his ten. He wants to put us in lounges . . . *lounges!* Opening for guys who sing "Feelings" and play the accordian.
JERRY: "The Buddy King Show," Tommy.
TOM: Lounges don't pay more than a thousand a week. Our take-home after taxes'll be less than three hundred each. Then you've got to pay living expenses.
JERRY: I don't want to hear this!
TOM: And you get paid in chips, man. Casino chips. Sure you can cash them in but it's a *long* walk through the casino to the cashier's window and I know you, Jerry. You'd never make it past the blackjack tables.
JERRY: Oh, you know me real good, don't you? So good you can fuck up the best chance of my life. Well, you don't know *shit* about me, Kelly. You don't know the way my gut *aches* to get on the "Buddy King Show." "Another young comedian, and another young comedian, and a bright and funny young comedian . . ." but never *us!* *Me!* Twenty million people!
TOM: Jerry . . .
JERRY: Shut up! I've waited for that night all of my life it seems. Because sitting out there in America in some perfectly pathetic domestic situation . . . sitting in their ugly, drunken fat . . . is every mother fuckin' sonofabitch who ever shit on me! They're all out there! Married to each other drowning in hopelessness. Watching *me!* On televisions that aren't even paid for yet! Watching *ME!* The ones who tormented and teased and humiliated me. The bitches who giggled behind my back! Their boyfriends who stole my lunch money! The fuckheads who called me Jew-boy! You know what's going on with them now?! Their lives add up to *zip!* There's Jerry Goldstein on the "Buddy King Show" . . . Their lives add up to *less* than zip. It's Jerry Goldstein.
TOM: Boy, will *they* be sorry. . . .
JERRY: Damn right. Wonder what they'll all do.
TOM: They'll probably kill themselves.
JERRY: I could dig that. I want to do that show, Tom.
TOM: I know. And we will someday.
JERRY: I want to do it . . . now!
TOM: The price is too high, Jerry.
JERRY: Don't stand in my way.

TOM: I'm right beside you. You just can't see me.
JERRY: [*Gestures with pen.*] I want you to sign this and I want you to sign it right now.
TOM: Who are you? Have we met? You look a lot like my partner.
JERRY: Sign this.
TOM: No way.
JERRY: Your last chance. Sign it or else.
TOM: Is being pathetic an Olympic sport yet? If it is you should try out for the team.
JERRY: You signing?
TOM: Read my lips: no fucking way!
JERRY: Get out.
TOM: What?
JERRY: I said get out.
TOM: Get out of where?
JERRY: Get out of *here*! My dressing room! Get out of my dressing room!
TOM: You're crazy.
JERRY: We're through! I'm sick and tired of this shit! You're holding me back! We're through! Get out of here!

[JERRY *throws a childish tantrum and begins throwing* TOM's *personal articles toward the door.* TOM's *hat, coat, briefcase all go flying at the door.*]

TOM: What are you doing!!!
JERRY: OUT!!! GET OUTTA HERE!!! GET . . . OUT!
TOM: Stop!!!
JERRY: Do this to ME?!! Do a thing like this to *ME*!! Who the fuck you think you are?!! You are NO ONE!!!

[TOM *dashes at* JERRY *and pins him against a wall.* JERRY *loses none of his rage.*]

TOM: Stop it!!!
JERRY: GET OUT!!!
TOM: Stop!!!
JERRY: AIN'T SHIT!!!
TOM: [*Slaps his face.*] Stop!!
JERRY: HATE YOUR FUCKIN' *GUTS*!!
TOM: [*Slaps his face.*] Stop! [*Slaps his face.*] Stop! What are you crazy? Who sat up with you in Atlanta when you thought you were going to die? Who? You so coked up you can't remember? You remember a hundred and five fever? Who stayed up with you for two days and nights? Was it Buddy King? Was it Sal? Who got his jaw broke in Pittsburgh? You thought it'd be funny to call some guy a "dumb fuckin' Pollock"! Turns out he was! Who got his jaw broke?!! Who was it!!! A few minutes ago you were ready to burn Sal for ever!

Work the city, find a new agent. Burn the old one! Now you want to burn me? Just like that? Is it that easy? Is it? IS IT?!! Are you in there? ARE YOU IN THERE SOMEWHERE?!!

[TOM *waits for a reply. There is none. After several beats he lets go of* JERRY *and slowly crosses to gather his belongings.* JERRY *gathers himself and crosses to the table where he takes a drink and sits down. He takes one of the the pens and finds a napkin on the floor, picks it up and prepares to make notes on the napkin.*]

JERRY: Okay. No problem here. I'm going to do the "Buddy King Show" on my own. That's what I'll do. I'm going to take all the bits I thought up . . . do 'em on my own. Make a list here. Write them down just like you do. "Tom's a writer . . . the brains of the team . . ." Hah! You don't write. You *type!* Make a list . . . all our bits. Work solo and do the bits I thought up. I'm takin' my bits, Kelly. And I'm writing new ones. Brand new bits . . . make a list . . . yeah.

TOM: You didn't forget?

JERRY: What?

TOM: On stage tonight. You didn't forget the new material?

JERRY: I'll write funnier stuff than *that!*

TOM: You were scared. I saw it in your eyes, Jerry. It was time to launch into the new material on stage. You took a beat, stammered around then jumped into the old material. The safe stuff. The stuff we've done a million times. And I said to myself "Holey shit! He's scared . . ." It was all over your face, man. You had the same expression you have right now.

JERRY: I'm going to send you a color TV, Kelly. A great big one. You can watch me kill on the "Buddy King Show." Alone. Without you.

TOM: Yeah, sure. You do that.

JERRY: I will.

TOM: Looks like you've got everything you need. Your paper and pencil . . . yourself . . . Your inspiration. Ooops, almost forgot. Your reason. Gotta have a reason, Jer.

[TOM *finds the cassette recorder and brings it to the table where he sets it down.*]

Can't do comedy without a good, solid, realistic reason. Here.

[TOM *presses the play button on the recorder. We hear the same wild audience applause and whistles we heard before.* JERRY *listens to the machine expressionless.* TOM *surveys* JERRY *for a few beats then sadly exits.*

Lights slowly fade to black.]

TRIPLET

(Awarded A National Endowment Grant)

(from the collection, TRIPLET)

by
KITTY JOHNSON

(The play was first presented at the Los Angeles Actors' Theatre's Festival of Premieres in 1982.)

Original Cast
(In Order of Appearance)

BRIDE . . . . Janet Carroll
VIRGIN . . . . Diane Tyler
PRINCESS . . . . Pamela Segal

Directed by . . . . Lee Rose
Produced by . . . . Adam Leipzig & Diane White

Bill Bushnell, Artistic Producing Director

[*The action takes place in the bedroom of the* BRIDE. *There should be three distinct areas within the room—one for each of the three characters. While these areas are home bases, the characters are free to move into areas assigned to the other two. The* BRIDE's *space is the focus, and contains a dresser, a pack of tarot cards, a bottle of champagne and a clay statue in progress. The* VIRGIN's *area contains the bed, several unopened birthday presents and her notebook. The* PRINCESS's *area should contain her dolls.*

At rise, BRIDE *is the only character in motion, just finishing her face and costume and preparing to go out.* VIRGIN *is in a frozen position, about to toast herself with a glass of champagne. She wears a letter sweater over her costume.* PRINCESS, *also frozen, is in the middle of telling an adventure story to one of her dolls, Aphrodite, who is dressed in blue.*]

BRIDE: Perfect. Absolutely perfect. You don't look a day over . . .
VIRGIN: [*Unfreezing*] Twenty-one!
BRIDE: . . . . thirty-one?
VIRGIN: Legal at last!

[VIRGIN *begins to open her presents. A horn honks outside and* BRIDE *rushes to the window.*]

BRIDE: Down in a minute!
PRINCESS: [*Unfreezing*] . . . .so she really got creamed by the tornado, and it plopped her down on top of this prehistoric animal that everybody else thought was extinct. But she wasn't afraid of anything, so she hopped on its back and rode to a buried pyramid. It was all dark and yucky and she didn't have any batteries for her flashlight . . .
BRIDE: [*Searching*] Something old . . .
PRINCESS: She found a secret light switch and, what do you know, there were all these people there! They yelled "Surprise!" and then they gave her all these neat birthday presents with her name on them. She got a box of water colors . . . and a record player . . . and a strapless bra . . . and all this make-up . . . [*She eyes* BRIDE's *make-up and moves to her area to experiment.*]
VIRGIN: Great. Cotton underpants with the days of the week on them.
PRINCESS: Whoever made up a law that says just because you play with dolls you can't wear lipstick on your thirteenth birthday is full of crap.
BRIDE: Fuck.
PRINCESS: [*Yells off-stage*] No, mother. I'm not using swear words. [*To herself*] Bitch.
VIRGIN: [*Opening next gift*] A circle pin?
VIRGIN & BRIDE: Wonderful.

BRIDE: Something old. [*She takes circle pin from* VIRGIN, *puts it on*]
PRINCESS: "Crap" is not a swear word. Neither is "fuck." "Jesus H. Christ" and "God damn it to hell". Those are swear words.
VIRGIN: [*Opening next gift*]: "Sex and the Single Girl."
PRINCESS: Neat!
VIRGIN: Oh, swell.
PRINCESS: Can I see? [*She snatches book from* VIRGIN]
BRIDE: [*To* VIRGIN] This is how far you've progressed in eight years?
PRINCESS: We have to get signed permission from our parents to study this stuff in school. Can you believe it? I mean everybody knows about sex.
VIRGIN: Do you mind?
PRINCESS: Some of these pictures are really weird. I'm not sure I ever want to get married.
BRIDE: Best idea I've heard today.
VIRGIN: [*Writing in her notebook*] "Everybody does it."
PRINCESS: I'm going to be a nun like Audrey Hepburn. Or maybe a helicopter pilot or a mortician.
BRIDE: Something new . . .
PRINCESS: You don't think I'll end up being a whore, do you?
BRIDE: You should live so long.
PRINCESS: My best friend Carolyn Newberry says I have the perfect makings of one. I saw this guy I like—Bobby Ferguson—in the cafeteria today and . . .
BRIDE: [*Surprised*] You know Bobby Ferguson already?
PRINCESS: You should see him. He's in the tenth grade and he's really cute, and I told him it was my birthday and he kissed me. So just because I let him, that doesn't make me a whore, does it?
VIRGIN: Of course not.
PRINCESS: She says that when you go all the way, it feels just like sliding down a firepole. Can you believe it?
VIRGIN: Who said that? I don't remember any Carolyn Newberry.
BRIDE: Miss Peroxide?
PRINCESS: I mean first of all, how would she know for sure unless she's done it herself, and second, who in the world would want to go around sliding down firepoles all the time? Unless you're a fireman or something.
VIRGIN: Oh, yeah. Carolyn Newberry.
PRINCESS: That's not really what it feels like, is it?
VIRGIN: You're asking the wrong person, kid.
PRINCESS: Of course, I know it would be a little different because you'd probably have a boy there with you and everything and I would never actually do it until I'm married and everything. . . .
BRIDE: Want to bet?

PRINCESS: I was just wondering what it feels like.
BRIDE: I've done it. And sometimes I wonder what it feels like, too.
PRINCESS: God, you're kidding. You've really done it? And the boys don't make fun of you or anything? They still like you?
VIRGIN: [*Writing*] "Cons: want respect."
BRIDE: [*Reading* VIRGIN's *book*] Is this the latest? "Pros: Chuck can't wait." Chuck? "Horny. Everybody does it." What's the matter? You're finally tired of being called a cock-tease?
VIRGIN: Who calls me that?
PRINCESS: I don't get it. What's a cock-tease?
BRIDE: I'd love to sit here and explain it to both of you, but I'm running a little late.
PRINCESS: Are you going to a birthday party?
BRIDE: Sort of. I'm getting married. I think.
PRINCESS: Wow.
VIRGIN: It's about time.
PRINCESS: Wait a minute . . . you're getting married on your birthday?
BRIDE: I need something new.
VIRGIN: The story of your life.
BRIDE: For the wedding? Something old, something new . . .
PRINCESS: You can't get married on your birthday! I'll get gypped out of extra presents. Everybody'll just give you one thing and say it's supposed to be for your birthday and your anniversary put together.
BRIDE: Gee. I never thought of that.
VIRGIN: How many times have you been engaged? Five?
PRINCESS: Engaged five times?
BRIDE: Seven.
PRINCESS: Just like a real heartbreaker. That's neat.
VIRGIN: And you're really planning to go through with it this time?
BRIDE: [*Showing tarot cards*] The tarot cards say that, karmically, this is probably the best time in my life for me to get married.
PRINCESS: Can you tell fortunes with these?
BRIDE: Besides, seven's my lucky number.
PRINCESS: But where's the long white dress? And the train and the veil and all the flowers?
VIRGIN: That's kid stuff.
PRINCESS: But I always wanted to get married someplace famous like the Wisconsin Water Mills and have four bridesmaids dressed in periwinkle and a flower girl and fuchsia gloves to match the rosebuds in my bouquet and my picture in the paper and everything.
VIRGIN: Or elope in the middle of the night and send a telegram to mom and dad from Paris—signed with my new name.
PRINCESS & VIRGIN: Don't you remember?
BRIDE: You're lucky I'm getting married at all.

VIRGIN: I see your point.
PRINCESS: How many kids are you going to have?
BRIDE: I'm not quite the mother type, honey.
VIRGIN: Don't embarass her, Sara. After all, she's got, what, two, maybe three years left before the odds get really ridiculous.
PRINCESS: You mean because she's so old, the kids'll probably come out deformed or retarded or something? [*She demonstrates, with a certain relish, by twisting* BRIDE's *clay statue-in-progress.*]
VIRGIN: Assuming she can even conceive.
BRIDE: You want to give me a break? I know how old I am.
PRINCESS: Oooh. This is neat.
BRIDE: [*Noticing* PRINCESS *at the statue*] Sara! How could you do that?
PRINCESS: I'm sorry. I was just playing.
BRIDE: Do you know how long I've been working on that? I almost had it right this time and now you've ruined it.
VIRGIN: She said she was sorry.
BRIDE: You're so busy talking about that stupid Bobby Ferguson, you don't even care what you do to somebody's art.
VIRGIN: [*To* PRINCESS] She doesn't mean it, Sara. You know how she over reacts to everything when she's on her period. Oh, God. Don't cry. Please. I hate it when you cry.
PRINCESS: I'm not crying.
BRIDE: I was going to give it to Eliot for a wedding present.
PRINCESS: [*Perking up*] Eliot?
VIRGIN: Eliot?
PRINCESS: Your boyfriend's name is Eliot? That's who you're getting married to?
VIRGIN: Eliot!
BRIDE: Something wrong with his name?
PRINCESS: I bet he has pimples. All the boys with dumb names always have pimples.
BRIDE: He does not have pimples and he happens to be very attractive. Take a look for yourself. He's right outside.
VIRGIN: No, thanks. I'd rather be surprised.
PRINCESS: Is he a millionaire?
BRIDE: Not yet.
PRINCESS & VIRGIN: [*Disappointed*] Oh.
PRINCESS: Does he at least buy you presents and things?
VIRGIN: What is he? A stockbroker? A tax attorney?
PRINCESS: Movie star?
BRIDE: If you must know, he drives a truck.
VIRGIN: Oh, God. I can't take it.
PRINCESS: What did he buy you for your birthday?
BRIDE: Close your eyes. I'll show you.

VIRGIN: A truck driver!
PRINCESS: They're closed.

[BRIDE *finds a pearl necklace and displays it for* PRINCESS.]

VIRGIN: Those went out of style about three years ago.
BRIDE: They're back.
PRINCESS: [*Non-committal*] They're pretty.
BRIDE: Look real close and you can see how all the pearls are just a little different. Can you tell?
PRINCESS: Sort of.
BRIDE: They used to be just little grains of sand in the ocean in Japan, see, and they went to visit these oysters and got caught inside and that's where they grew up to be pearls.
PRINCESS: Wow!
VIRGIN: Great story.
BRIDE: And not a single one of them is perfect.
PRINCESS: Oh.
BRIDE: But that's good.
VIRGIN: Sure.
BRIDE: That's how you can tell they're real.
PRINCESS: You mean the perfect ones are fake?
BRIDE: You remember that, okay?
PRINCESS: God, they're so pretty.
BRIDE: You'd really like Eliot. He drives all around the country in his truck and he makes up songs while he's . . . of course! Something new! [*She puts on pearl necklace.*]
PRINCESS: Do you guys do it?
BRIDE: Don't you ever think about anything but sex?
PRINCESS: You're not allowed to think about it?
BRIDE: Exclusively?
VIRGIN: At least all we do is think about it.
BRIDE: At least I'm not frigid.
VIRGIN: Look. I just don't want to get pregnant. Okay?
BRIDE: So take your birth control pills. Let me get them for you. How long have you had these? Have you opened the case yet? Do you even know what color they are?
PRINCESS: They come in colors?
VIRGIN: I can't believe how much you've changed.
BRIDE: Sweet Sara grows up into cold-hearted slut?
VIRGIN: I didn't say that.
BRIDE: You never commit to anything, do you?
VIRGIN: I'm just disappointed.
BRIDE: Don't be. I'm not.
VIRGIN: You're not serious?

BRIDE: Hey. Take a look. I've done almost everything on that damn list of yours. I've been to Paris, Egypt, Greece. I've sold paintings. I'm independent.
PRINCESS: Yeah. It's not like she's an old maid or anything.
BRIDE: Thank you.
VIRGIN: I suppose lots of people are starting to get married late in life.
BRIDE: Late in life? I'm thirty-five years old. I'm in my prime. Eliot's in his prime, too. Intellectually.
VIRGIN: An intellectual truck driver?
BRIDE: Truck drivers are very important people. The economy would collapse without them.
VIRGIN: Forget it.
BRIDE: Is that what you say to the boys after you get them in heat? Forget it?
VIRGIN: You are so bitter.
BRIDE: Not bitter, sweetheart. Just more experienced in the ways of the world than you. More sophisticated. More mature.
VIRGIN: Is that why you're marrying a truck driver? Because you're more "mature"? Or is he just your last chance?

[*The horn honks again outside.* BRIDE *wavers between snapping at* VIRGIN *and going to window. She opts for the latter.*]

PRINCESS: What's wrong with her?
VIRGIN: Probably change of life.
BRIDE: [*Out window*] I'm on my way.
VIRGIN: I feel sorry for her.
PRINCESS: You want to play with me and Josephine?
VIRGIN: Josephine. Empress of Napoleon.
PRINCESS: Or we could do something else if you want.
VIRGIN: You decide.
PRINCESS: We should do something really neat 'cause it's our birthday. You get to do whatever you want on your birthday.
BRIDE: If you've got the guts.
VIRGIN: [*Ignoring* BRIDE] You think so?
PRINCESS: God, are you kidding? Last year when I was twelve, I smoked two Camel cigarettes and mixed up some Seven-Up and sloe gin and drank the whole thing. I didn't even barf.
VIRGIN: That's revolting.
PRINCESS: This year I'm going to have a party. But not tonight 'cause it's a school night.
VIRGIN: That's the same reason I'm not out tonight.
BRIDE: Ha. Ha. Ha.
PRINCESS: I know! We can tell a story!
VIRGIN: No, thanks.

PRINCESS: I know a really neat one about a girl who lives in Blanchester.
VIRGIN: I think I've heard this one before.
PRINCESS: No, wait. It's about a princess. I forgot. There's this beautiful princess . . .
VIRGIN & PRINCESS: . . . and her name was Sara.
PRINCESS: She was so pretty and so smart and everybody liked her a whole lot. She was a ballerina and a homecoming queen and a meteorologist and she stayed up late every night. And she had a maid to wash her dishes.
VIRGIN: Right. And one day on her way home from Paris, she decided to go on this safari because she'd only been to Africa once before and . . .
BRIDE: Africa? You know what they have in Africa? Diamond mines. They're way under the ground and filled with these big blue rocks. So they crush the rocks and . . . look! Diamonds! [*She shows* PRINCESS *her engagement ring.*]
PRINCESS: Is that your engagement ring?
VIRGIN: So. She was in Africa, see, while all her friends were stuck back home in Blanchester at their boring nine-to-five jobs and they never got to travel around the world like she did. . . .
PRINCESS: Yeah! And she got lost in the jungle and got captured by these horrible cannibals who boiled her in this pot of water with lizards and maggots in it.
BRIDE: I wonder if Eliot has ever been to Africa?
VIRGIN: But it started to rain and the fire under the pot went out.
BRIDE: How exotic.
VIRGIN: And she was so pretty that even when she was soaking wet, she looked just like Marilyn Monroe.
PRINCESS: And this King came along, and he fell madly in love with her. . . .
VIRGIN: Of course!
PRINCESS: . . . and they moved to this little island in Greece. . . .
BRIDE: You want to cool it with the Prince Charming stories?
VIRGIN: We don't know any truck driver stories.
PRINCESS: I think I might invite Bobby Ferguson to my party Saturday. He says I'll probably grow up to be a famous artist. Do you think that means he likes me?
VIRGIN: Now I remember. Bobby Ferguson. I wonder what ever happened to him.
BRIDE: He got his head blown off in Viet Nam.
PRINCESS: Sick.
VIRGIN: You're kidding.
BRIDE: Right. I'm kidding.
VIRGIN: That was real funny, Sara.

PRINCESS: Did they serve it on a platter? Like St. John the Baptist?
BRIDE: Can you shut her up?
VIRGIN: You're the mature, sophisticated woman of the world. Little thirteen year old girls shouldn't bother you.
PRINCESS: [*To* VIRGIN] You want to play with Cleopatra? She's much more sophisticated than Josephine.
VIRGIN: Cleopatra. Queen of the Nile. I think I'll go to Egypt after Paris. [*She writes this in her notebook.*]
PRINCESS: I don't see why you didn't like your presents. I think they're really neat.
VIRGIN: I'm twenty-one years old. I just signed a contract for my first teaching job, and I still get presents for a thirteen year old.
BRIDE: What did you expect? Black negligees and a bottle of My Sin?
VIRGIN: Maybe.
BRIDE: Better learn what to do with them before you start asking for them.
VIRGIN: Don't you have someplace to go? Isn't that semi out there blocking traffic?
BRIDE: Oh, God. Eliot.
VIRGIN: [*To* PRINCESS] You're right. It's my birthday. I can do whatever I want. [*She starts to dial phone.*]
BRIDE: [*At window*] Ten minutes! I promise!
PRINCESS: I thought we were going to play.
VIRGIN: I'm going to play. Grown-up games. Okay? I'm going to play with Chuck. [*She changes her mind, does not complete the call.*]
PRINCESS: Then why did you hang up?
VIRGIN: I'm going to call him. I just need to relax a little first.
BRIDE: Isn't that what he's supposed to tell you?
VIRGIN: You make it sound like I'm the only twenty-one year old virgin on the planet.
BRIDE: If you're saving it for Mr. Right, honey, you've got a long wait.
VIRGIN: I want to do it. Really.
BRIDE: [*Taking* VIRGIN's *notebook*] Let me write that down for you. "Want to do it. Really." Is that a pro or a con?
VIRGIN: I just don't want to plan it, you know?
BRIDE: "Must be spontaneous."
VIRGIN: But if I don't plan it, I'll probably end up doing it in the back seat of Chuck's Corvair and that is so tacky.
BRIDE: "Can't be tacky."
VIRGIN: I want . . . sheets . . . and maybe a little . . .
BRIDE: . . . soft music . . . a . . .
BRIDE & VIRGIN: . . . fireplace . . .
VIRGIN: . . . or something. I just want the . . .
VIRGIN & BRIDE: . . . first time to be perfect.
PRINCESS: The perfect ones are fake.

BRIDGE: [*To* VIRGIN] She catches on faster than you do.
VIRGIN: And I want to be sure we're really in love.
BRIDE: Please. Spare me the details.
VIRGIN: What would you know about love? Miss Stand-em-up-at-the-altar?
BRIDE: I certainly know more about it than Chuck whatever his name. . .
VIRGIN: Cooper.
BRIDE: Cooper. Right. Played football or something?
VIRGIN: He's captain this year.
BRIDE: [*Dryly*] Wonderful.
VIRGIN: And he organizes peace rallies, too.
BRIDE: And he stands you up on your twenty-first birthday.
VIRGIN: He had to study.
BRIDE: Right.
VIRGIN: But look. He gave me his letter sweater and fraternity pin.
BRIDE: Check the pockets.
VIRGIN: [*Checking pockets*] God. What a slob. [*She finds various odds and ends, including a pack of rubbers, which she throws across the stage toward the* PRINCESS.]
PRINCESS: Hey, what's that?
BRIDE: Rubbers.
PRINCESS: [*Picking them up*] Yick.
VIRGIN: Creep.

[VIRGIN *angrily takes off the letter sweater, snatches* BRIDE's *champagne bottle and pours herself a drink as she writes in her book.*]

BRIDE: Help yourself.
VIRGIN: It's my birthday. I can do whatever I want.
BRIDE: Do you know what you want? Without looking at the list?
VIRGIN: I just want things to turn out like they're supposed to once in a while. Is that too much to ask?
BRIDE: If you really want to know, we can ask the cards.
VIRGIN: You don't actually believe in that stuff?
BRIDE: Beats making lists.
VIRGIN: Lists help me sort things out, okay? They help me plan my future.
BRIDE: Is that so?
VIRGIN: Look. Over here are my short-term goals and then I have my long-range plans in the back. Then, on the opposite side, I write down my reasons for wanting certain things to happen, so when I start changing my mind, I can always go back and remember why I made the decision in the first place.
BRIDE: Does this mean you are actually making decisions now?
VIRGIN: For example, I want to go to Paris to study art, right? I mean

two separate professors have told me I'm the most gifted abstractionist they've seen in centuries. I still need discipline and everything, but that'll come as I get older.
BRIDE: I certainly hope so.
VIRGIN: So, under long range goals, I write: Paris. It takes a lot of money to go to Paris, so obviously I can't do it right away. So now I have to figure out: how do I get the money?
BRIDE: Beats me.
VIRGIN: All I know about is art, so-o . . . I teach it. That's a short-range plan.
BRIDE: Fascinating.
VIRGIN: I think it is. I went back to Blanchester High over Spring vacation and the principal remembered me and he offered me this position teaching art to seventh and eighth grade, which will be really neat because that's when I first started getting really into it. So I teach there for three years, save all my money and move to Paris.
BRIDE: You're sure you wouldn't rather learn how to read these cards?
VIRGIN: I guess I'll have to change my plans with Chuck, though. [*She rips his page from her book.*]
BRIDE: You'll have to change a lot more than that.
VIRGIN: God, I don't understand. My own boyfriend, my own boyfriend, who says he loves me and respects me and wants to marry me is walking around campus with rubbers in his pockets.
BRIDE: You'll get over it.
PRINCESS: Maybe he was saving them for you. [*She snaps one of the rubbers across the stage to* VIRGIN]
VIRGIN: Grow up.
BRIDE: Stoping playing with those. [*She takes the rubbers from* PRINCESS.]
PRINCESS: Now she's crying.
VIRGIN: I'm not crying.
PRINCESS: How come she's allowed to cry and I'm not?
VIRGIN: This is the last time anybody does this to me. This is the last time anybody hurts me.
BRIDE: I don't think so, Sara.
VIRGIN: Every time as soon as you let somebody know you care about them, they go out of their way to see how much they can hurt you.
BRIDE: Or they die on you. Like Bobby Ferguson.
VIRGIN: [*Writing in book*] Hmmm. Bobby Ferguson.
PRINCESS: Is that a list of your boyfriends?
VIRGIN: Not exactly.
BRIDE: The broken-hearted virgin makes another list. What is it this time? Whichever jock gets the highest score gets to fuck you? You don't think that's a bit juvenile? Or calculating?
VIRGIN: You call *me* juvenile and calculating? You're the one who plays

with fortune-telling cards and you keep Eliot out there waiting while you make up your mind if you can lower yourself enough to marry a truck driver and . . .
BRIDE: I never said he wasn't good enough for me.
VIRGIN: Then why aren't you outside in that truck?
BRIDE: You're saying all the wrong things. It's our birthday. We're supposed to be nice to each other on our birthday.
PRINCESS: I'm being nice.
BRIDE: You? You're the one who ruined the present!
VIRGIN: [*To* BRIDE] You're as much of a baby as she is.
PRINCESS: I'm not a baby. I'm a teenager.
VIRGIN: All that make-up doesn't make you an adult, Sara.
PRINCESS: And I suppose you're all grown up just because you don't cry.
VIRGIN: I'm certainly more grown up than you are.
PRINCESS: Then how come you don't even have the nerve to call a boy on the phone?
VIRGIN: Calling boys is immature.
PRINCESS: It is not. I called Bobby Ferguson last week.
BRIDE: Fuck.
VIRGIN: I bet.
PRINCESS: I did.
VIRGIN: You did not.
PRINCESS: I did too!
VIRGIN: I bet he hung up on you.

VIRGIN: Perfect! Bobby Ferguson!
BRIDE: No! Don't!!

PRINCESS: Did not!
VIRGIN: Okay. Then what did he say?
PRINCESS: Don't know. He wasn't home.
BRIDE: The present isn't right, I can't find something borrowed and I talk to dolls. There's a law someplace that says if you talk to dolls, you're not ready to get married. I want to do it. Really. We could go on those long hauls together and I could sketch while he was driving and he could play his guitar while I was driving . . . How can I ever become a famous artist if I'm tied down like that?
PRINCESS: I'm not ever going to be tied down. I'm going to be my own woman.
BRIDE: [*To* PRINCESS] Such a pretty doll.
VIRGIN: Are you all right?
BRIDE: I am fine! This is the happiest fucking day of my life. Or it would have been if you and your tear-jerking rubber stories hadn't fucked it up for me.
VIRGIN: You mean Chuck?
BRIDE: No!
VIRGIN: You wanted to marry Chuck?
BRIDE: Only weak-willed insecure birdbrains marry their college sweethearts.
VIRGIN: But if you had married him, while you were still young and everything, then you could have experienced that first and gotten it out of your system and gone to Paris and done all those other things later, after your kids had grown up and you were divorced and everything.
BRIDE: Have you got all that written down on one of your famous lists?
PRINCESS: I'm going to Paris first and fall in love with somebody there.
BRIDE: I met Eliot in Paris.
PRINCESS: Neat. Did he kiss your hand like in the movies?
BRIDE: Did I ever tell you what he did? He learned how to open a pack of matches with one hand and strike the match with his thumb without even taking it out of the folder. In case he got an arm shot off in Viet Nam. No. That was Bobby. Bobby did that. I was supposed to marry Bobby. I had it all written down in the book. He was going to be famous, too. We were both going to be famous and live in Paris and have these two kids—first a boy and then a girl. And a maid to wash the dishes.
VIRGIN: You're allowed to make changes in the book, Sara. You can rip out whole pages, even.
BRIDE: I can't. [*Again, the horn honks outside.*] Do me a favor. Go tell Bobby . . . I mean Eliot . . . go tell Eliot I can't get married today. He'll understand. I'm just not ready.
VIRGIN: No. Let's think this out logically. . . .
PRINCESS: You have to get married. Everybody gets married.

BRIDE: Not everybody. Not me.
VIRGIN: But you said yourself it was perfect timing. You're more mature now. You've seen the world, you've slept around . . . and it's not like Eliot wants you to give up your career or anything.
BRIDE: Career? What career? I was the most gifted abstractionist they'd seen in centuries and here I am. Back in Blanchester. Teaching again. The only thing I change more often than jobs is lovers.
VIRGIN: That's just because you're above falling into a rut. That's great.
PRINCESS: Yeah. That's great.
VIRGIN: So now you can marry Eliot. . . .
PRINCESS: . . .and live happily ever after. . . .
BRIDE: No. It doesn't work like that.
VIRGIN: But it does if you go about it right. Here. You can borrow my book. Just write down all the things you want and . . .
BRIDE: Will you stop with that book? Do you know how many things you'll miss out on because it's not written down in that stupid book?
VIRGIN: Miss Independent Strong Will Fortune Teller. You think you're so mature just because you're older than me and tell me to go out and get laid and make fun of me because I don't want it to be cheap or I want to be selective about who I do it with. But you! You're real brave. You're terrified of even getting married. You won't take a chance on anything.
BRIDE: You've got it all figured out, haven't you? You know it all. You're so fucking careful all the time. You color in all the little squares and everything will be perfect. But what happens when you go outside the lines, Sara? What happens when you find out life isn't a paint-by-numbers kit?
PRINCESS: Kits are for retards. I want to paint like a real artist.
BRIDE: What is that, I wonder. A real artist?
VIRGIN: It's not too late, Sara. It can still be perfect. It can be.
BRIDE: Don't you ever listen to anything? The perfect ones are fucking fake. There is no such thing.
VIRGIN: For you, maybe. But I've got my whole life in front of me and I can do whatever I want with it. I'm never going to let myself become like you. Never.
BRIDE: Good idea.
PRINCESS: This new eyeshadow is great, Aphrodite. I was getting so tired of orange. I was just telling Bobby Ferguson—he's my fiance, you know—how he's got to stop kissing me in the cafeteria. If he wants to make out, it'll have to be someplace perfect where there's music and candles and stuff. I hope I didn't hurt his feelings, though. You know how Bobby is. He overreacts to everything when he's on his period. I think I'll call him again. [*She puts her hand to her ear, as if she were holding a telephone receiver and listens to the "ringing."*]

VIRGIN: When I'm twenty-three, things are going to be so different. I'll probably be living in Greenwich Village or London or someplace really exotic where no one has ever heard of Blanchester. I'll sell my paintings on the beach and I'll have lots of boyfriends who won't want to sleep with anyone else in the whole world except me. And I'm gonna be so-o sexy.
BRIDE: You don't understand. Bobby wasn't supposed to die. He was the fucking cameraman for the goddamn news. He wasn't supposed to die.
PRINCESS: [*Hanging up phone*] He's never home. Shit.

[*Again, the horn honks outside.*]

BRIDE: Fuck.
VIRGIN: [*To* PRINCESS] You've got it made.
PRINCESS: Yeah. I do?
VIRGIN: Goodbye Mr. Snot Nose Chuck-the-Jock. You're not the only one who knows how to have a good time. [*She goes through her book to find a name.*] Perfect! Bobby Ferguson!
BRIDE: No! Don't!
VIRGIN: Why not? I'm not going to fall in love with him or anything. I'm not going to fall in love with anyone until I'm twenty-seven.
BRIDE: Here. Take the rubbers back to Chuck. Call Chuck. He's probably great. He's an athlete. Athletes are great in bed. And what about Paris? This is great. Listen. Move to Paris right after graduation! Something. Just don't call Bobby Ferguson. Please.
PRINCESS: Once upon a time, there was this beautiful princess and her name was Sara. She grew up and had big boobs and repainted the Sistine Chapel. And she had dates with lots of cute boys who all wanted to marry her right away.
BRIDE: But she was a princess, so she couldn't marry just anybody.
VIRGIN: [*Having dialed phone*] Hello? Bobby Ferguson? You probably don't remember me. You weren't home the last time I called.
PRINCESS: So one day after she invented the cure for cancer, she was walking down the street . . .
BRIDE: She never invented anything, Sara. Except stories.
PRINCESS: She was good, though, wasn't she? A good artist?
BRIDE: Oh, yes. She was very good. Just not quite . . .
VIRGIN: Perfect! I'll see you in about an hour.
PRINCESS: So, she was this really good artist and she met this millionaire movie star who fell madly in love with her.
VIRGIN: [*To* BRIDE] Bobby Ferguson! Remember at the football games in high school how he would always pass the ball to somebody else so he wouldn't get tackled? No wonder he never made captain.
BRIDE: Bobby Ferguson did no such thing.
VIRGIN: No. I definitely remember him now. Blond, with the chipped

tooth. Used to leave those disgusting green things that look like vomit under the teachers' desks.
BRIDE: Bobby? Bobby did that?
PRINCESS: He throws spitballs, too. He's really funny.
BRIDE: Spitballs?
VIRGIN: A long way from Mr. Right, but he might be kind of fun.
BRIDE: You two must be thinking of someone else. Bobby was . . .
PRINCESS: Perfect!
VIRGIN: I hardly think so, Sara. Unless his sense of humor has improved.
BRIDE: Not really. He used to sit on the bed and clip his toenails and try to stack them up like building blocks. He could really be a jerk sometimes.
VIRGIN: A nice guy, though.
BRIDE: Yeah. A nice guy.
VIRGIN: Like Eliot?
BRIDE: Like Eliot.
PRINCESS: So-o, even though she wasn't really sure she could marry a movie star, she fell in love with him anyway, 'cause he was a really nice guy and he sang songs while he drove. . . .
BRIDE: Eliot. . . .
PRINCESS: And he gave her this great big diamond ring that had pearls in it and you could tell they were real because not one of them was perfect. . . .
VIRGIN: [*Taking one of her birth control pills with champagne*] You can do whatever you want on your birthday. If you want to.
BRIDE: If I really want to . . .
PRINCESS: . . . and they sailed away on his truck and she made him into a King, and he made her into a movie star. . . .

[BRIDE *takes* VIRGIN's *notebook, rips out some of the pages.*]

VIRGIN: What are you doing?
BRIDE: Just getting rid of some of the fairy tales.
VIRGIN: But what will you replace them with?
BRIDE: Let's be surprised.

[VIRGIN *toasts* BRIDE *and freezes in her original position.*]

BRIDE: [*Indicating circle pin, pearls*] Something old, something new. . .

[PRINCESS *offers* BRIDE *her Aphrodite doll.* BRIDE *takes it.* PRINCESS *freezes in her original position.*]

BRIDE: . . . something borrowed . . . something real.

[*She goes to meet Eliot.*]

JUNK FOOD

by
WILLARD MANUS

(The play was first presented at the Los Angeles Actors' Theatre's Festival of Premieres in 1981.)

Original Cast
(In Order of Appearance)

She .... Carole Goldman
He .... Richard Edelstein

Directed by .... Richard Edelstein
Produced by .... Adam Leipzig & Diane White

Bill Bushnell, Artistic Producing Director

Junk Food

[TIME: *Late night.*

PLACE: *A garbage dump on the outskirts of a large city.*

With the curtains closed, we hear the sound of a car coming close, passing us, stopping and backing up. Through the curtains we will see the glare of the car's headlights.

When the curtains open, there is the car, headlights blazing, tape deck blaring music. Ideally, the car should be something special, a custom-built convertible. But the play can also be done with blocks. We are in a garbage dump. A circle of light should surround the car, with darkness beyond. Perhaps we can see a suggestion of the distant city—the twinkle of a few street lights, a red neon glow. No garbage or junk should be seen on stage. In the car are a couple, out on a date. She's wearing a bouffant wig, and maybe a bright green sweater and skirt. He's got on a pair of corduroy jeans, a sports shirt, and a basketball jacket.

HE *turns off the headlights.* THEY *sit for some moments listening to the music.* SHE's *stirring around in her seat, looking round unhappily—disbelievingly—at the garbage dump.*

SHE *leans forward and turns off the music.*]

SHE: You're really bringing me here?
HE: What's it look like?
SHE: You must be some kind of jerk. It stinks.
HE: You'll get used to it.
SHE: [*Disgustedly.*] We're surrounded by garbage!
HE: Today it's garbage. Tomorrow it's condos.
SHE: What a disgusting thought—condos with their feet stuck in shit.
HE: Hey, watch your mouth. Around here they call it landfill. [*With a gesture.*] Look around you . . . what do you see?
SHE: An old peed-on mattress . . . an icebox . . ."No Trespassing, Violators Will Be Prosecuted." C'mon, we'd better get out of here; we'll get arrested.
HE: Take it easy! It's safe, believe me. [*Beat.*] You ever been arrested?
SHE: Once.
HE: For what?
SHE: Drunken driving. You?
HE: Twice.
SHE: What for?
HE: Punching out creeps.
SHE: Nice. You do any time?
HE: Once, for three months. Wasn't bad. I learned a lotta good things inside—how to smoke dope, hotwire a car, fuck faggots.

SHE: Got yourself a regular college education. [*Peering sideways at him.*] You really like it here?
HE: [*Moving close and slipping an arm round her.*] Why not? It ain't so bad, once you get used to the smell. Nobody around—no cars, no cops. And no Peeping Toms either . . . [*Making a light pass.*] We can do whatever we like here, dig?
SHE: [*Pushing him away.*] Don't get any ideas. I hardly know you—[*Screaming suddenly.*] There's a rat! A rat!

[*Grabbing a .22 rifle from beneath the front seat,* HE *stands, aims, fires a shot at the rat.*]

HE: Got him! Got the sucker!
SHE: [*Pointing*] There's another!
HE: [*Firing again.*] Damn, I missed!
SHE: [*Horrified.*] Did you see the size of it? Big as a rabbit.
HE: That's nothing. I've seen 'em big as dogs.
SHE: Christ, let's get out of here!
HE: [*Sitting atop the car seat, rifle in his arms.*] Hey . . . Make believe you're on a safari, hunting lions in Africa.
SHE: Fuck the lions! Take me home.
HE: Not until I bag a few more.
SHE: You are weird, man.
HE: Shut up and try to understand. I'm a man, I need to kill. But what am I gonna do, kill people? They'll put me back in jail for that. So I gotta kill animals. But where . . . in the mountains? I ain't got the time or money. At least here I got sport, action . . . and it don't cost me a dime.
SHE: King of the Rats!
HE: Why not? It beats bowling or watching TV.
SHE: When I met you this morning, I didn't figure you'd turn out like this.
HE: How'd you figure I'd turn out?
SHE: I don't know. Crazy . . . but in a normal way.
HE: Well look again. I ain't "normal." [*Grinning proudly.*] I'm a Great White Hunter. You want a beer?
SHE: If it's Lite.
HE: [*Sliding down into seat.*] Tonight I got what you want.

[*From the back seat ice chest,* HE *brings out a Lite beer for her, a dark one for himself.* SHE *turns the music on.*]

SHE: This car of yours is really something. I never went over a hundred miles an hour before.
HE: Told you I had some horses under this hood. You liked the ride, huh?
SHE: I did, even though I almost tossed my cookies, honey. [*Beat.*] You got something to go with this?
HE: Yeah, me!

SHE: No, I mean like Frito's Corn Chips.
HE: From the bandito! [*Hands her the Fritos.*] You know what my biggest fear is? That this Princess of mine should die before I do. God forbid she should end up here one day, rotting away on some junkpile.
SHE: It'll never happen. Not the way you take care of it.
HE: [*Eyeing her.*] You know something, you're some dancer. . . .
SHE: [*Pleased.*] You think so?
HE: [*Slipping an arm over her seat.*] I know so. You really turned me on at the disco.

[HE *makes another pass. She doesn't fight him off at first—is even tickled by it—but has to shove him away when he gets too eager.*]

SHE: [*Struggling with him.*] Don't rush me—don't rush me— [*Exasperatedly,* HE *turns off the music and sits back, wiping the lipstick off his mouth. Then* HE *grabs his rifle and stands again, peering into the darkness with an angry scowl.*]
HE: Come on, you rats, show your beady little eyes! [*Spotting one,* HE *fires at it.*] One! [*Another.*] Two! [*Another.*] Three!

[*With a whoop of triumph,* HE *sits down again, still holding the rifle in one hand, but making another pass at her with the other. Pulling her close.*]

Come on—let's do what we came to do!
SHE: [*Wrestling with him again.*] Not so fast, I hardly know you! [*Grabbing the rifle from him,* SHE *stands and points it at his groin warningly.*] Bang, bang!

[HE *laughs painfully and slowly reaches up and takes the rifle away from her.*]

HE: You want me to show you how to shoot it?
SHE: You mean it? I've never fired a rifle before.

[*Getting out of the car,* HE *crosses in front of it, beckoning to her.* SHE *gets out and stands in front of him, downstage right.*]

HE: [*Snuggling up against her.*] Tuck it against your shoulder . . . hold the stock, not the barrel . . . wrap your finger around the trigger and squeeze it gently. [*Aiming it for her.*] There's one!
SHE: [*Terrifiedly.*] Eeeek!
HE: Shoot!

[*She fires the rifle with his help.*]

SHE: Did I hit anything?
HE: Yeah . . . an old tailor's dummy. [*Pointing.*] Christ, there's another one! [HE *helps her to fire again.*] Wow! You blew him away!

[HE *heads back to the car, putting the rifle down by his side again.*]

HE: Them rats may be the only things to survive an atomic blast. You and me, we're gonna get sauteed in radiation but them rodents out there are gonna thrive on it; they're gonna multiply by the millions and take over the world! [*Angered by the idea,* HE *grabs his rifle again and stands up in the car, aiming it at the rats.*] See that fat, slimy one over there? He'll probably be President one day! [*Shooting.*] Come back, you fucking politician! You bandit! Racketeer!
SHE: [*Upset.*] Hey, cowboy, take it easy. You'll get a heart attack. [*Pulling him down.*] Sit down, cool off. [*Looking at him.*] What're you so mad about? What's all the screaming for?
HE: [*Genuinely surprised.*] Was I screaming?
SHE: You shoulda heard yourself. Regular opera singer.
HE: Sorry. [*Switching music on.*] I'm makin' a great impression, huh?
SHE: What's eatin' you?
HE: I don't know—nuthin'.
SHE: Nuthin, he says, sitting in the middle of a garbage dump.
HE: I told you, I like it here. I'd rather be here than in that goddamn foundry we go to every day.
SHE: It's a job.
HE: It's a racket! You paid your dues this afternoon, didn't you? [*She nods.*] You know where that money goes?
SHE: Into our pension fund.
HE: Bullshit! [*Switching music off.*] It goes right to the bigshots and they put it out on the street.
SHE: I don't understand.
HE: They shylock it, dummy! They put it out at 40 per cent and get fat off the proceeds.
SHE: [*Shocked.*] Our union's ripping us off like that?
HE: [*Sarcastically.*] Hey, look, the pussycat's wakin' up!
SHE: That's not right, it's not fair! It's our money, not theirs.
HE: You tell 'em, honey. You tell 'em that and see what happens.
SHE: [*Defiantly.*] I'm not afraid.
HE: Oh, no? Then try talkin' back to them like I did today.
SHE: What happened?
HE: When the shop steward put out his hand for my dough, I squawked. I told him I didn't think the union was givin' us a fair shake. You know what he did? He took out this knife, about yea long, and said, "Hey, man, another word outa you and I'm gonna carve you out a new asshole."
SHE: You did something, didn't you?
HE: [*Bitterly.*] Sure, I did something. [*Beat.*] I handed over the money!

[*Upset,* HE *jumps up again and begins firing the rifle rapidly and wildly at the rats.*]

HE: Bastard. Slimy bastard! Fucking shop steward! Bandit! [HE *empties the rifle, then slumps back down in his seat, spent, downcast.*

SHE *looks at him with compassion in her eyes. Finally . . .*]

SHE: Hey . . .
HE: What?

[*Taking the rifle from him,* SHE *leans across and places a kiss on his lips.* HE *manages a grin.*]

You always hold a man's gun when you kiss him?
SHE: Only when it's loaded.

[*That prompts him to make another pass.* HE's *all over her now, grabbing and pawing.* SHE *pushes him away, roughly.*]

Not so fast, take it easy. I hardly know you.

[*Irked,* HE *lets go of her and climbs out of the car.*]

HE: [*Angrily.*] You're a stuck record. "I hardly know you—hardly know you—"
SHE: Well, it's the truth.
HE: Whadda ya hafta know me for? You close your eyes when you make love, don't you? So what's the difference who's on top of you?
SHE: [*Standing and getting out of the car.*] Are you serious? You think I'm going to screw a stranger?
HE: You don't have a choice!
SHE: Sez you.
HE: C'mon, admit it. You'll never know me and I'll never know you. I can't even figure out the guys I work with. Eight hours a day, five days a week, fifty weeks a year—and they're still a mystery to me. What the fuck are they doing there, working that dumb miserable job? What *am* I doing there?
SHE: Making a living, that's what.
HE: [*Hotly.*] That's not what I'm talkin' about! I don't know shit about them, they don't know shit about me, so how could I know anything about you?
SHE: [*Quietly.*] Haven't you ever been close to somebody?
HE: Yeah . . .[*Patting the car.*] . . . you're sitting in her lap right now.
SHE: [*Disgustedly.*] You're sick! You're very, very sick in the head.
HE: I'm not sick—just honest. I feel closer to this baby than I ever did to any human being.
SHE: Oh, bullshit! You just don't have the guts to open yourself to somebody.
HE: If I did, you couldn't stand it—
SHE: I can stand anything.
HE: Not what's inside me.

SHE: What's inside you that's so terrible?
HE: Garbage.
SHE: Garbage?
HE: You heard me. Just think about it. We been eating crap from the time we were born. Think of all the lies your parents ever told you. What'd you ever get out of church except that religion smells like a two-thousand-year-old fart! The only honest thing I learned in school was how to jerk off. And from then on the movies and TV took over. Jesus, you talk about bullshit! All those phony hospital and cop shows are mouldering inside me like rancid cheese! If I opened my mouth wide, I'd smell like a dump-truck! If you could see the inside of my head, it'd look like a Tijuana cat-house!
SHE: It's all so negative with you. You look at white and see black.
HE: It's better than lookin' at black and seein' Technicolor!

[HE *drinks again, this time fishing out a bottle of Jack Daniels and swallowing from it, followed by a chaser of beer.*]

SHE: [*Watching him.*] You always drink like that on a date?

[HE *doesn't answer.*]

Hey, I asked you a question.

[HE *finishes the beer, crumples the can in his fist and tosses it away.*]

HE: I don't like talking to idiots.
SHE: Idiot . . . ? *I'm* an idiot? You got it all wrong, mister. *You're* the fucked-up one, not me.
HE: Yeah, yeah, you're terrific. You got a healthy mind in a healthy body.
SHE: Compared to you, that's right.
HE: You make me laugh, you know that? There ain't a real thing about you, yet you sit there smug and self-satisfied as a lawyer.
SHE: What's fake about me?
HE: For starters, your hair. It's made of horse hide, or maybe even horse shit!
SHE: Shut your disgusting mouth!
HE: [*Relentlessly.*] It's true, ain't it . . . you don't have a real hair showing on your head.
SHE: I've never worn a wig!
HE: [*Reaching out.*] Let me see—
SHE: [*Pulling away.*] What?
HE: I said let me see—
SHE: No!

[*To escape his reach,* SHE *jumps out of the car.* HE *follows her out momentarily.*]

HE: You see, it's always the same. You're afraid you'll be found out.

[SHE *stomps back to the car and clambers into her seat.*]

SHE: Take me home!

[HE *returns to the car, switching on the headlights in getting ready to leave.*]

HE: You're like everyone else . . . afraid someone'll come and lift up the lid.
SHE: And you? You're perfect, of course, just like Mother Nature made you—except for your pearly whites.
HE: What are you talking about? [*Turning off the headlights.*] What have my teeth got to do with this?
SHE: I watched you in the lunchroom once, eating a sandwich. Something got stuck in your gums. Out came that bridge of yours. You've got a mouth like a hockey player's!

[*That shuts him up.*]

Well, what have you got to say now? Nothing!
HE: Leave off, willya—
SHE: You're the one who's so honest about everything—except when it comes to yourself.
HE: I've got nothing to hide.
SHE: Prove it! Take out that bridge of yours.
HE: If you'll take off your wig.
SHE: Agreed! Tit for tat, fella—that's my philosophy.
HE: Mine, too.
SHE: Then go ahead—my hair for your teeth.
HE: You really mean it?
SHE: I knew you didn't have the guts.
HE: Sez who?
SHE: Sez me!
HE: [*Finally.*] Tit for tat, huh?
SHE: Yeah, tit for tat!
HE: And then?
SHE: Then we'll see.
HE: What are the rules?
SHE: We'll make them up as we go along. [*Beat.*] Scared to play?
HE: With you? No way.
SHE: Then go ahead. Start.
HE: You first.
SHE: You!
HE: You!
SHE: Chicken! First you promise, then you run—just like a man!

[*They stare at each other. Finally, with a sign of surrender,* SHE *reaches up and removes her wig.*]

All right, there it is! Your turn, sport.

[HE *laughs at the sight of her scrawny natural hair, but turns away and, shielding his mouth, removes his upper bridge.*]

HE: [*Grinning*] Like a garden rake, huh?

[THEY *both laugh.*]

SHE: [*Touching her hair.*] Like a dish of spaghetti!

[HE *reaches out and runs a hand over her hair.*]

HE: You may look like your grandmother, but real hair feels nice.

[*Now* SHE *reaches out and runs her hands through his hair.*]

SHE: Teeth or no teeth, you still got a nice smile.

[*All of a sudden* SHE *gives a cry as something comes away in her hands.*]

My God—what is this? You got a scalp disease or something?
HE:[*Sheepishly.*] I had a hair transplant. You're holding two weeks pay in your paws.
SHE: [*Laughing.*] You and me, babe. I blew a hundred and fifty smackers on this wig!

[*Laughing too,* HE *clowns around by taking her wig and clopping it atop his head.* SHE *gives another raucous laugh and snatches it away from him. Silence.* THEY *look at each other, connecting.*]

HE: [*Intently.*] How come you came here with me?
SHE: What do you mean? You asked me out.
HE: But how come you're free? A woman like you—the way you dance and all—you should have a regular guy by now.
SHE: I told you this morning, I like to play the field.
HE: That's bullshit, and you know it.
SHE: Maybe I don't want a regular guy!
HE: C'mon. You wouldn't of gone out with me if you didn't want a man. [*Scrutinizing her.*] You ever been married?
SHE: Yeah . . . almost.
HE: What's that mean?
SHE: [*Painfully.*] I was supposed to get married a couple of months ago.

[SHE *switches on the tape deck.* HE *turns it off.*]

HE: So what happened?
SHE: Two nights before the wedding I found my fiancé fucking an old girlfriend of his.
HE: Ah. . . . forget him.
SHE: I try, I really do. That bastard! I thought he was the greatest. [*Beat.*] You know what happened this evening? He comes up to me and

looks me in the eyes and whispers how much he misses me and wants me. You talk about bullshit! That lying son of a bitch manufactures it!
HE: [*Reaching for her compassionately.*] Hey . . .
SHE: [*Pulling away.*] Don't! [*Beat.*] Come on, come on . . . tit for tat!
HE: You're sure you want to?
SHE: Why the hell not?

[THEY *stare at each other, hard. Then* HE *shrugs and begins bringing out whatever things* HE *has in his jacket pocket.*]

HE: All right, then. My junk for yours. [*Throwing things away, one by one.*] A pair of sunglasses . . . a nail file . . . a comb . . . a movie ticket stub: "Pussycat Theatre." Hell, did I really pay five bucks to see a dirty movie? [*Rips it to pieces.*] . . . a handkerchief . . . a lighter . . . some change . . . a pack of gum . . . [*Shooting her a look of consternation at what* HE *finds next.*] . . . and . . .
SHE: [*Going after him.*] What is it? What've got in your hand?
HE: [*Trying to hide it.*] You wouldn't be interested. [SHE *chases him around the car.*]
SHE: C'mon, show it!

[*Catching him from behind,* SHE *twists it out of his hand. It's a packet of condoms. One look at it and* SHE *throws it to the ground with a little snort of disgust.*]

You're a pig!
HE: A pig's someone that doesn't care if he knocks up a girl. Therefore, I ain't a pig!

[*Putting his hands in his jacket pockets,* HE *feels around.*]

That's about it.
SHE: Let me see your jacket.

[HE *takes it off and hands it over.* SHE *checks out the label and looks questioningly at him.*]

"Magic Man?"
HE: Magic Johnson.
SHE: The basketball player?
HE: [*Sheepishly.*] Yeah.
SHE: What else have you got of his?
HE: [*Showing a sneakered foot.*] Magic Johnson Converse All-Leather sneakers.
SHE: [*Laughing.*] Anything else?
HE: Yeah, yeah . . .
SHE: What?

HE: [*Indicating back seat of car.*] Back there . . .

[SHE *goes round and picks up a bag of cookies from back seat.*]

SHE: [*Reading from label.*] "Magic Johnson Chocolate Chip Cookies." [*Shooting him a disapproving look.*] You oughta be ashamed of yourself, a grown man like you!

[SHE *flings the bag away.* HE *goes for her handbag, digging around in it.*]

HE: C'mon, let's go on. Let's go on, dammit!
SHE: [*Getting out of the car.*] Hey, be careful, there's money inside.
HE: Ah, I see—if it comes to money, we gotta stop.
SHE: I didn't say that. It's just that, well, shit, I'm no millionaire.
HE: Tit for tat, remember? This bag feels like it's loaded with gold bars.

[HE *starts pulling magazines out of it and flinging them away.*]

"Real Romances." "Secret Romances." "Intimate Romances." [*Looking at her.*] You got romance on the brain?

[*Beginning to report on other objects* HE *finds and tosses aside.*]

"Costa Brava, the cologne from Spain." [*Sniffing it.*] Smells like Spanish Fly! [*Next object*] "Elizabeth Arden Sunshine Red Lipstick." It ain't lipstick, it's war paint! [*Next.*] "Eterna Cream with Progenitin." What the hell is this, did you rob a drugstore?

[SHE *has been chasing him round the car all along, trying to wrest the bag away from him.*]

SHE: A girl's gotta make herself pretty!

[SHE *makes another move, which* HE *dodges.*]

HE: "Estee Lauder's Lotus Patina Eyeliner". . ."Estee Lauder's Soft Film Compact Bronze". . . [*Confronting her.*] Tell me, who is this Estee Lauder—a relative of yours?
SHE: [*Peevishly.*] Do you hafta read all that out?
HE: [*Holding up a small jar.*] "Jada Eyelashes—Makes You Sexy—" [*Showing empty jar.*] Empty. . . .
SHE: Those lashes are where they're supposed to be.

[HE *suddenly goes to her, reaches up and yanks her false eyelashes off.*]

HE: I'll show you where they're supposed to be!
SHE: Ouch! Shit, that hurts!
HE: That'll teach you to cheat! Here I was lookin' at you and thinkin'—man, what beautiful sexy eyes this chick has. What's the reason? [*Singing.*] Jada, jada, jing, jing, *jing.*
SHE: So I wear false eyelashes, what's the big deal? Linda Evans advertises them on TV.

HE: You're not Linda Evans.
SHE: And you're not Magic Johnson!

[HE *roots around in her handbag again.*]

HE: What else have you got in here? [*Coming up with her wallet.*] How much money you got?
SHE: About twenty-five bucks.
HE: [*Throwing wallet away.*] Fuck money!
SHE: —hey!
HE: —it's the root of all evil!
SHE: Is that right? Then prove it! Gimme yours.

[HE *hands her a wad of bills.*]

HE: Done. Go ahead, get rid of it!
SHE: [*Taken aback.*] Listen . . . you must have a hundred bucks here . . .
HE: [*Shouting.*] Get rid of it, I said!
SHE: You mean it?

[*When* SHE *sees* HE's *serious,* SHE *starts running around the car, shedding bills this way and that, and laughing giddily, excitedly.*]

All right! All right!
HE: [*Cheering her on.*] Get rid of it. . . . Get rid of it all! All this crap that's choking us to death!

[*Dumping the rest of the contents of her bag out,* HE *finds a packet of her personal photographs.*]

HE: I don't believe it! [*Indicating one of the photos.*] The Pope? You really carry a picture of him wherever you go?
SHE: Why not? I love him.
HE: You love your Master, huh? He tells you what to do and think and you love him for it.
SHE: I don't care what you say. I think he's cute!
HE: [*Astounded.*] Cute? The Pope is cute? How could he be cute: He's Polish!

[*Takes photo and rips it up into small pieces.*]

SHE: [*Angrily.*] For that you'll burn in Hell for all eternity!
HE: Great! It'll be a big improvement over this! [*Looking from next photo to her.*] Your Mother? [SHE *nods.*] Wow . . . what a battle-ax.
SHE: You're right! Tear it up! [*Pointing to the next one.*] But not that one! That's my dog Sundance. He loves me.
HE: Stop feeding him and you'll see how much he loves you! [*Tearing that one up,* HE *comes to the next.*] What about this one?
SHE: No, be careful, that's my daugh— [*Hurriedly.*] I mean, my niece.
HE: Let's get it straight. Who is she—your daughter or your niece?

SHE: [*Finally.*] All right, it's my daughter.
HE: Figures. Where's Poppa?
SHE: He disappeared sixteen years ago.
HE: Went out for a pack of cigarettes, huh?

[HE *makes as if to tear up the next photo.*]

    This one I don't believe.
SHE: Why not?
HE: The Pope, OK. Your Mother, even your dog, all right . . . but an autographed photo of *Barbara Walters*?
SHE: I think she's wonderful!
HE: [*Tearing photo to shreds.*] I think she's a sourpuss!
SHE: [*Angrily.*] OK, wise-ass. You're so superior, let's see *your* photos.
HE: [*Handing wallet over.*] Be my guest.
SHE: [*Looking at first photo.*] Who's this Marine? [*Sudden realization.*] Hey, it's you—look at all those medals—

[HE *grabs the photo and rips it up himself, savagely.*]

HE: To hell with the fucking medals! Anybody who was in Viet Nam should shut up about it. He should wear black and come out only at night!
SHE: [*Taken aback, stares at him.*] Did you kill anyone?
HE: I came back, didn't I?

[SHE *gives a shrug and goes on to the next photo . . . and the others after that.*]

SHE: Harriet . . . Gertie . . ."Love, LuAnne." [*Making a face.*] Ugh, Agnes! [*Looking across at him.*] What are you, a lady-killer? Mr. Macho Man? [*Checking other items off.*] . . . driver's license . . . social security . . . pay stub. How much you make?
HE: The money's still buggin' you, isn't it?
SHE: You sure you don't want to pick it up? Think of all the good times we could have with that bread. . . .

[HE *has come close and is rubbing up against her, suggestively.*]

HE: I'm having a good time right now.
SHE: You really mean it? You really want to go all the way?
HE: Gettin' cold feet? Wanna quit?
SHE: No, you?
HE: I'll see it through. Go ahead!
SHE: OK.

[*Digging into his packet again,* SHE *finds a clipping.* HE *winces when* HE *sees it and, turning away, returns to his car seat.*]

[SHE *reads what the clipping says.*]

Junk Food

"Swinging Scandinavia's best-selling adult books are now available at popular prices. You must be 21 years of age and over to certify. Send now for your free brochure." [*Looking at him reprovingly.*] What's this . . . you read Scandinavian literature?
HE: [*With a sigh.*] Only the pictures.
SHE: [*Going to him.*] How come you need such things?
HE: I stopped havin' girl friends.
SHE: Prefer to be alone?
HE: I felt alone even when I was with them.
SHE: [*Tentatively.*] Do you feel alone with me?
HE: [*Staring at her.*] Now? No . . . how about you?
SHE: I feel OK. Yeah, really OK. [*Tossing photo packet aside.*] I'm finished.

[SHE *walks away from him.*]

HE: I'm not. [*Gives her a whistle, holding out his hands.*] C'mere.

[SHE *wheels around instantly and goes to him, putting her face down for what* SHE *thinks will be a kiss.* HE *kisses her, all right, but at the same time plucks her earrings off and tosses them away.*]

SHE: O-w-w-w!
HE: Christmas is over! It's time to strip the tree!

[*Jumping out of the car,* HE *grabs her arm.*]

We're getting down to the nitty-gritty.
SHE: [*Trying to pull her arm away.*] No—not my watch!
HE: Give it!
SHE: [*Quickly.*] It's an underwater watch—Swiss—cost me nearly two hundred bucks.
HE: Underwater? What in hell do you need with an underwater watch? Are you a deep see diver? Jacques Cousteau's mistress? I'll bet you can't even swim?
SHE: [*As* THEY *wrestle for the watch.*] I'm learning at the Y!
HE: [*Wresting it away.*] Well, you can learn without your watch on! [*Flinging it away.*] There! Now the rats can tell what time it is.

[*Silence.* THEY *face each other.*]

SHE: Your turn.
HE: Not quite. [*Beat*] Hand over your ring.
SHE: Wait a minute—not my ring.
HE: Why not?
SHE: It's the only valuable thing I own. It's worth a coupla hundred bucks—
HE: Give it!
SHE: No!

HE: C'mon, there's no quitting now—
SHE: Oh, please!
HE: Give it! Show your guts!

[SHE *looks from the ring to him and back . . . and finally takes it off and hands it to him.* HE *shakes no.*]

You!

[*A last look at the ring, before bringing it to her lips and giving it a farewell kiss. Then* SHE *chucks it away.*]

SHE: I did it!
HE: That's right, you really did!
SHE: [*Looking around with a little smile.*] We're sure getting there.
HE: Yeah, we're getting cleaned out . . . just like an enema.
SHE: [*Beat*] Except for your car.
HE: [*Shocked.*] My car!
SHE: [*Scornfully.*] Not your car, huh? Anything but your car.

[HE *can only put a hand out and touch his car, protectively, lovingly.* SHE *watches him.*]

You're in love with a car, a goddamn box-on-wheels!

[HE *has been rendered speechless.*]

What's the matter? Lost your tongue?
HE: [*Finally, in a choked voice.*] You know how much time I spent fixing her up?

[SHE *suddenly gives the car a kick.*]

SHE: [*Tauntingly.*] You're in love with a machine, a thing without a soul!

[*Again* SHE *kicks the car, beats on it with her fists. Enraged,* HE *goes for her.*]

HE: [*Shouting.*] Stop that! Just stop that!

[SHE *eludes him by scurrying round the other side of the car.* THEY *face each other on opposite sides of it.*]

SHE: [*Beating up on it again.*] Like hell I will!
HE: Wait a minute now—just wait a minute!
SHE: Can't stand to have anybody touch her, huh? You know what—
    I'll bet you wash this thing more'n you wash yourself.
HE: Oh, yeah? Well, don't be such a wise-ass!
SHE: [*Kicking at it again.*] I can just see you fussin' over it—spendin' all
    your free time on it—
HE: [*Screaming.*] Enough!

HE: Tuck it against your shoulder . . . hold the stock, not the barrel . . . wrap your finger around the trigger and squeeze it gently.

[SHE *stops and stares at him, relentlessly.*]

SHE: Had it? Afraid to go any further?
HE: [*Tightly.*] I got about ten thousand bucks tied up in that Queen.
SHE: Oh, yeah? Well, what was it you said before about money?

[HE *looks at her, then at the car.* SHE *goes toward him.*]

Admit it. You don't have the balls to go all the way.
HE: [*Outraged.*] I don't?
SHE: No, you don't!
HE: [*Past all words.*] I don't? I don't have the—!

[*The blood pounding in his face,* HE *stands with his mouth working, but no sound coming out. Finally,* HE *is able to gain enough control to speak, hoarsely.*]

Stand back now. Just stand back, damn you!

[*Going to the rear of the car,* HE *opens the trunk and drags out a set of snowchains. (Note: The action here can be done strictly with sound and mime.)* HE *comes round and stands by the side of the car, staring down at it. Perhaps* HE *gives it a last fond, apologetic caress.*]

Sorry, Queenie. . . .

[*Then, as* HE *raises the chains up over his head, the stage lights go to red or blue. Time the lights and sound as* HE *lashes out with the chains and starts attacking the car, bashing away at it with all his might, again and again. We hear the sound of metal and glass being broken up, smashed apart, in a kind of symphony of destruction as* HE *attacks the car from every angle now, shouting at the top of his lungs.*]

HE: How am I doin'? Like my music?
SHE: Yeah—it's beautiful!
HE: Then c'mon—help me bust her open—rip her guts out!
SHE: [*Giddily.*] All right!

[SHE *joins in the trashing of the car by grabbing whatever* SHE *can from it—cans of beer and soda, boxes of crackers, the ice chest, etc.—and flinging these things aside, whooping and shouting all the while.*]

Yippeee!
HE: Yeah!
SHE: Do it!

[*The two of them really get into it, shouting and screaming in primal fashion as* THEY *smash the car to pieces. The destruction should go on for several long moments, culminating in a complete and final purge of emotions.* SHE *is the first to drop, exhausted and out of breath, near the* car. HE *breaks off soon after, flushed and sweating, but in a state of exaltation.*

The lights go back to normal, but are much softer in intensity. The two of them are bathed in a dim but warm light, a beautiful light. Long pause as THEY *try to catch their breath. Finally* THEY *can speak.*]

SHE: So . . .
HE: . . . yeah . . .
SHE: . . . wiped out . . .
HE: Me, too. [*Looking at car.*] Jesus, did I really do that? I must be crazy.
SHE: We both are.
HE: The work I put into that thing.
SHE: But that's all it is—a thing.
HE: [*Grabbing her.*] . . . c'mon . . .
SHE: We're going on?

[HE *pulls off his shoes.* SHE *does the same.*]

HE: Hey, you're short!
SHE: I wear wedgies.
HE: You're practically a midget.
SHE: You shouldn't talk, with your pirate's body.
HE: My what?
SHE: Pirate's body—all sunken chest! Hah, hah!

[*Things are going fast now.* SHE *is pulling off her blouse,* HE *his pants.*]

SHE: [*Flinging blouse away.*] Here, junk-pile, here's a K-Mart special for you!
HE: [*Doing same with trousers.*] And a pair of Calvin Kleins!

[SHE *points to him giggling.*]

SHE: Look at you—what funny underwear.
HE: [*Sheepishly.*] Magic Johnson boxer shorts. But if you think that's funny, look at this! [*Yanking open his shirt.*] Like it? [HE'*s wearing a corset to hold in his belly.*] Like what you see? [*Pulling corset open and tossing it aside.*] Ever seen a better beer belly?
SHE: [*Laughing.*] You look like a Japanese wrestler!
HE: Your turn now. Take it off!
SHE: Turn around!

[*As* HE *does,* SHE *quickly reaches into her bra and pulls out either some bust pads or cotton wadding.*]

HE: [*Catching her in the act.*] Hah! Caught ya! No tits, huh?
SHE: [*Removing her bra.*] Who said? They just don't stand up the way they used to.

[SHE's *got her arms crossed over her breasts to hide them.* HE *gestures for her not to.*]

HE: [*Truthfully.*] That's all right—they're nice—I like 'em just the way they are. . . .

[SHE *drops her arms. Near-naked.* THEY *look at each other. Pause.* HE *indicates* SHE *should remove her panties.* SHE *indicates* HE *should do the same with his boxer shorts.* THEY *come to a mutual, silent agreement to do it together. With their backs to the audience,* THEY *wriggle out of their underwear, turn and face each other with their hands protecting and hiding their private parts.*

THEY *look at each other again. With a little movement of his hand—or even a finger—*HE *suggests* SHE *should go first.* SHE *does the same back to him.*

Time it so that THEY *both remove their hands and expose themselves at the same time.*

THEY *look at each other, warmly, acceptingly.*]

SHE: [*Finally.*] Disappointed that I don't have a *Playboy* bod?
HE: That's OK. . . . I don't have a *Playgirl* cock.

[THEY *stare at each other again.*]

SHE: [*Finally.*] We did it!
HE: Yeah, we sure did. [*Beat.*] You know something?
SHE: What?
HE: You're ugly . . . but you look terrific.
SHE: Same to you.
HE: [*Reaching out for her.*] C'mere. . . .
SHE: [*Teasingly.*] Catch me!

[HE *tries to grab her, but* SHE *dodges away.* HE *chases her.* THEY *run round the car, laughing all the while. Finally,* HE *catches up with her and pulls her close.* THEY *embrace in a warm, loving, enfolding way. No words now . . . just soft cries of joy. Then* HE *pulls back.*]

HE: [*Pointing.*] You've got a birthmark. . . .
SHE: You've got a tattoo. "Sharon."
HE: Play your cards right and maybe I'll put your name there.
SHE: Is there something else I should know?
HE: Yeah . . . I've got fallen arches.
SHE: That's OK. I've got a deviated septum.

[THEY *embrace again. Then* HE *pulls back.*]

HE: There is one last thing I've got to tell you. . . .
SHE: What?

HE: [*Smiling.*] I voted for Nixon.
SHE: [*Smiling back.*] No problem! I never voted for anybody!

[*Another embrace, this time a deep, loving one. Then* HE *points.*]

HE: Look, there's a mattress over there. What say we put it to good use?
SHE & HE: [*Together*] But I hardly know you.

[SHE *laughs and takes his hand.* THEY *start off. Then* SHE *stops.*]

SHE: What about the rats?
HE: Oh, yeah. The rats.

[HE *crosses to car, picks up rifle, cocks it. Looks at her again.*]

    OK?
SHE: [*Smiling.*] OK.

[*Shouldering the rifle,* HE *takes her hand and* THEY *move off into the encircling darkness together, side by side.*

The lights fade down.]

ON A COLD AND FROSTY MORNING

(Winner of the Bellow Award, Cornell University)

(from the collection, ENDANGERED SPECIES)

by
JOSEPH SCOTT KIERLAND

(The play was presented at the Los Angeles Actors' Theatre's Festival of Premieres in 1981.)

Cast
(In Order of Appearance)

The Clown .... Joseph Della Sorte
Bella .... Joy Claussen
Bata .... Ken Foree

Directed by .... Gennaro Montanino
Produced by .... Adam Leipzig & Diane White

Bill Bushnell, Artistic Producing Director

[*Black. Wind. From the darkness comes the sound of a laugh—strange and dreamlike. The lights begin to rise very slowly on what appears to be three sleeping Figures hunched together for warmth under the cold howl of the wind.*

The strange laugh is coming from the one dressed in the Clown's suit and makeup. He abruptly stops his dreamy laugh to look up at the rising light. He sighs deeply—]

CLOWN: Ahhhhhhhhhh—at last it's riiiiiii-sing—it's riiiiiii-sing.

[CLOWN *nudges one of the Figures hunched with him.*]

The light, Bella— the liiiiiii-ght—

[BELLA *slowly wakes and lifts her head to squint into the growing light. She is wearing a bareback rider's costume and is also still in her makeup.*]

It's as if the Show was about to begin. Can you hear the Crowd? The animals sense it too. The light—and the orchestra—the orchestra.
BELLA: Do you see him?

[*There is a long silence as* THEY *stare out. The wind howls, and the light continues to rise slowly. The large man,* BATA, *stirs, and joins their long stare. He is wearing an old baggy suit, a tie, no shirt, but a high hat that he wears straight on his head, pushed down very tightly.*]

BATA: It snooooo-wed again last night.
BELLA: Do you see him?!
BATA: You can't see the road or the truck anymore. His tracks are gone too.
BELLA: The little Bastard isn't coming back.
CLOWN: Now, now, now—we know better than that, don't we, Bata? Nemo is trustworthy—!
BELLA: I never trusted him—!
CLOWN: You most certainly did. It was your idea to let Nemo go back to the truck. I remember it distinctly.
BELLA: I'm so goddamn cold and hungry. I didn't want to let that little Creep out of my sight—and I told you that.
CLOWN: Nemo is trustworthy. I'm almost sure of that.
BELLA: You can never trust a Dwarf! Dwarfs always work against you! How the hell do you think they survive in this World? If you could trust a Dwarf, he wouldn't survive.
CLOWN: You're being unreasonable again, Bella. Nemo probably just drove the truck down the mountain to get help.
BATA: He couldn't drive anywhere in all that snow.
BELLA: Aaaaaa—if the stinking little shit stood up on the seat he couldn't even look out the window.

CLOWN: He'll be back. I know he'll be back! He promised he'd bring food—and more clothes—
BATA: He did say that, Bella. I heard him say it. "I'll bring back food," he said. He definitely said that. "I'll bring back food!"
CLOWN: Of course he did—! And I'm certain he went to find the others! That's it—pure and simple! He went to find the others!
BATA: Sure—
BELLA: Then where the hell is he?!
CLOWN: Out there—somewhere, out there! And when he comes back—well then—we'll just get on with the Show—won't we, Bata?
BATA: Yes. And everything will be just like it was before!
CLOWN: Of course—of course—of course—
BATA: The Crowds of people and the colored lights going on and off—on and off—on and off—
CLOWN: And Bella will ride three— *four* new Horses at the same time while Nemo beats the big drum and crashes the cymbal on his head!
BATA: And I'll get every machine going at the same time for the celebration! The Carousel spinning round—the Wheel climbing up and up—! And the People laughing and shrieking—!
CLOWN: And the puppets—always the funny puppets!
BATA: Every machine at the same time—think of that!
CLOWN: And the calliope!

[*The* CLOWN *begins to dance with* BATA *and imitate the tooting oom-pah-pah of the calliope.* BELLA *has not moved from staring out toward the light, and she pays no attention at all when* BATA *and the* CLOWN *begin to sing.*]

BATA & CLOWN: All around the mulberry bush,
The mulberry bush, the mulberry bush,
All around the mulberry bush,
On a cold and frosty morning.

All around the mulberry bush,
The mulberry bush, the mulberry bush.

[*The* CLOWN *suddenly stops dancing. He sets himself and takes three imaginary balls out of his pockets. He begins to juggle the imaginary balls, and* BATA *applauds.*]

CLOWN: Announce me—announce me!!
BATA: Oh, I couldn't do that. Only Nemo can announce you!
CLOWN: Then give me a drumroll! Quick—quick!

[BATA *begins to beat an imaginary drum and make its rolling sound with his mouth.*]

Wonderful—wonderful!!

[*The* CLOWN *continues to juggle the imaginary balls, but then he misses and they scatter. The* CLOWN *moves awkwardly to retrieve his imaginary balls as* BATA *continues to beat his imaginary drum.*

The CLOWN *sets himself and again attempts to juggle the imaginary balls, but this time he has difficulty even getting started and the balls scatter.*

BATA *stops his drumming as the* CLOWN *again has to retrieve his imaginary balls.*]

BELLA: Hopeless Fool!
CLOWN: One day I'll juggle fifty-six balls like the Ugly Zorino.
BELLA: Impossible!
CLOWN: There's no such thing as impossible to an Artist. But what would you know about it? You're nothing but a Bare-Back Rider! You've never known the agony—the torture.
BELLA: Who the hell is the Ugly Zorino anyway? I never heard of him!
CLOWN: You see?! And she tells everyone she's been in the Carnival Business for twenty years.
BELLA: Ten years, that's all!
BATA: Noooooo—it's been more than that, Bella. Don't you remember we worked together in Denver that hot summer when you got all those saddle blisters on your ass?!
BELLA: Ten years—ten years—no more!
CLOWN: Listen to her! The Ugly Zorino's been around for generations. You can ask anyone!
BELLA: Never heard of him!
CLOWN: He worked the Florida Coast and did a flame swallowing act. But his genius was with the balls!
BELLA: Did *you* ever see him?!
CLOWN: Nemo worked with him!
BELLA: Nemo?! You can't believe a Dwarf!
CLOWN: Nemo always announced the Ugly Zorino with trumpets. Zorino demanded trumpets!
BELLA: There's no such thing as an Ugly Zorino!
BATA: And cymbals! I remember Nemo saying that—trumpets and cymbals!
BELLA: Nemo's a liar—he always lies!
CLOWN: Nemo steals a little—but he never lies—never lies—never lies!
BELLA: He's a stinking Dwarf that lies and steals!
CLOWN: He appreciates the Artist—and that's more than I can say for you!
BELLA: He's not coming back! That's how much he appreciates the Artist! Once we decided that we were going to do it, we should've never let him out of here!

CLOWN: He has to come back! Where else could he go?!
BATA: He's right, Bella! Nemo probably went to look for the others. The Great Romero and the Fat Lady were in the truck behind us. They have to be down there somewhere.
CLOWN: He'll bring us back some food—because he appreciates! That's why he offered to go!
BATA: And when he comes back he'll teach you to juggle fifty-six balls like an expert.
CLOWN: Like an Artist—a great Artist!

[BATA *and the* CLOWN *begin toot-tooting like a calliope again, and they dance about the stage taking mock bows.*]

BELLA: The Dwarf isn't coming back because he knew what we were going to do to him!

[BATA *and the* CLOWN *suddenly freeze in their dance, and only the howl of the wind circles them.*

BELLA *moves slowly to the edge again and speaks into the wind.*]

I can feeeeeeel him—smell him—taste him—somewhere near us.

[*The* CLOWN *suddenly calls into the wind.*]

CLOWN: Ne-mo—Neee-mooooo—! Neeeeeeeeee-moooooooooo!

[*The wind rises and fades with his call.*]

BATA: It's beginning to snoooow again!
CLOWN: Neeeeeee-moooooooooo!
BATA: Snooooow—Snoooooooow—
CLOWN: Neeeeee-moooooooooo!

[THEY *stare out waiting for an answer, but even the wind fades into silence.*]

BATA: Let's go down to the truck and bring him back.
BELLA: He doesn't want us to find him!
CLOWN: You mean he's playing Hide and Seek?
BELLA: He's not in the truck. He just waddled out there and sunk down into it! I could see it in his face! The little Bastard knew there was no food in the truck! He just made that up so we'd let him go. He knew what we were going to do with him. The little Bastard knew!

[*A long silence.*]

BATA: I knew there was no food in the truck.
CLOWN: Why didn't you say something?! Why did you let him go?!
BATA: There's nothing but heavy machinery in the truck.

CLOWN: And you knew all the time?!
BELLA: And so did Nemo!
CLOWN: You're both crazy! Nemo will be back before the light goes down. He's got to come back!

[*The* CLOWN *turns and moves back upstage to set himself for juggling the imaginary balls.*]

Give me a drumroll!

[BATA *and* BELLA *move upstage, but neither gives the* CLOWN *his drumroll. The* CLOWN *carefully takes the imaginary balls out of his pockets and begins to sing as he prepares to juggle the balls.*]

CLOWN: Sour grapes, sour grapes,
 All the Apes eat sour grapes,
 Pick a bunch, pick a bunch,
 And we'll have a picnic lunch.

Louder with the drumroll, Dummies!

[BATA *and* BELLA *just stare at him as he begins to arc his imaginary balls. One, two, three—but they scatter before he can even arc them a few times. The imaginary balls roll toward* BELLA *and she picks them up. There is a long silence as* THEY *watch* BELLA *with the imaginary balls.*]

BELLA: Give me the high hat, Bata!
BATA: My hat?
CLOWN: Give me back my balls!
BELLA: Give me the hat!
CLOWN: Don't do it, Bata! She's up to something!

[BATA *holds the high hat tightly on his head.*]

BATA: I'll give you the Ring Master's jacket if you want.
BELLA: The hat!
BATA: Take the Tattooed Man's tie!
BELLA: The hat!!
BATA: The Great Romero himself gave me this hat!
BELLA: Give me the goddamn hat!!!
CLOWN: She's got the balls! If she gets the hat, who knows what she'll do? She might even try to drive us out of the Carnival. She's an ambitious and ruthless Bare-Back Rider! You saw what she did to Nemo!!
BATA: What did she do to Nemo?
CLOWN: She made him go out in that storm! Can you imagine a Dwarf surviving in that storm? We should've stopped her!
BATA: She didn't make him go! He went by himself!
CLOWN: She'll do anything to get her way!

BELLA: Give me that hat, Bata!
BATA: You can't keep it!
CLOWN: Don't do it, Bata!
BATA: I always wanted this hat, and when the Great Romero gave it to me—
BELLA: We're just going to play a game with the balls.
CLOWN: Ahhhhhh—the truth comes out. She's trying to take the Center Ring! She wants your hat for the Horses to wear!
BATA: A lot of people in the Carnival have tried to steal this hat!
CLOWN: You can't trust a selfish and cruel Bare-Back Rider! She stole my balls—she'll steal your hat!
BATA: Nobody steals this hat!
CLOWN: You see?! You can't fool *him* that easy—and I'll get my balls back!
BELLA: Hold the hat!
BATA: Hold it?
BELLA: Take it off and hold it in your hand.

[BATA *slowly removes his tight-fitting high hat and holds it in his hand.*]

CLOWN: Be careful, Bata.

[BATA *grips the high hat tightly as* BELLA *moves toward him—and drops the imaginary balls—one by one—into his high hat.*]

BELLA: Green—Yellow . . .
CLOWN: My balls—my balls!
BELLA: . . . and Red. The one who picks the Red Ball takes the Dwarf's place!
CLOWN: No! Give me back my balls!
BELLA: If you don't pick—then we will! You'll take the ball that's left! Shake them up, Bata!

[BATA *reaches into the high hat and stirs the balls. Then he offers the hat to the* CLOWN. *The* CLOWN *is frightened and puts his hand into the hat, but suddenly pulls it back.*

BELLA *sneers at him and reaches quickly into the hat and chooses an imaginary ball that she hides behind her back.*

The CLOWN *slowly reaches out again. He is terrified and he closes his eyes as his hand sinks into the hat and comes out with one of the imaginary balls. He is afraid to open his eyes.*]

CLOWN: Which one is it? Is it the red one?!

[*Silence.*]

You vicious Bastards! It's the red one, isn't it?!

[*The* CLOWN *drops the imaginary ball and opens his eyes.*]

It's yellow—it's the yellow ball! I picked the yellow one! I picked the yellow one!!

[*The* CLOWN *realizes that* BATA *and* BELLA *are staring at each other—and* BATA *suddenly reaches into the hat and pulls out the last imaginary ball.*]

BATA: Green!

[*He is ecstatic, and the* CLOWN *laughs with him. Then* THEY *turn to* BELLA, *who is still hiding the last ball behind her back. She suddenly holds it out and says . . .*]

BELLA: Blue!

[*For a moment,* THEY *stand in awe of the event.* BATA *turns the high hat over, but there is nothing in it.*]

CLOWN: The red ball's gone—it's gone!!
BELLA: Gone where?!
CLOWN: It's a sign—a good sign!
BATA: It's the Great Romero's trick hat! It's magic!
BELLA: Don't give me that shit!

[BELLA *grabs for the high hat, but* BATA *pulls it away and jams it back on his head.*

The CLOWN *grabs his imaginary balls back from* BELLA *and* BATA *in the confusion.*]

CLOWN: The red ball has gone to Nemo—gone to Nemo—to Nemo—

> Sour grapes, sour grapes,
> All the Apes eat sour grapes,
> Pick a bunch, pick a bunch . . .

BELLA: Then we'll do it again without the red ball!!
CLOWN: Go get your own balls!

> Pick a bunch, pick a bunch,
> And we'll have a picnic lunch.

[*The* CLOWN *sets himself to juggle his imaginary balls again—looks over at* BELLA—*decides against it and puts his imaginary balls away.*]

BELLA: All right—this—time—we play Blindman's Buff!
CLOWN: [*Singing.*] Sour grapes, sour grapes . . .
BELLA: You're blind first!
CLOWN: We don't know how to play Blindman's Buff!
BELLA: I'll teach you!
BATA: Blindman's Buff is *my* favorite game.
CLOWN: I don't want to play—I don't want to play! He's the one it should be! Not Nemo—not you—not me! Him!! He doesn't belong

in the Carnival. He's an Outsider—a mechanic! We can find another mechanic anywhere—they're a penny a bunch—a penny a bunch—a penny a bunch! But how many great Bare-Back Riders are there? How many magnificent juggling Clowns? He doesn't belong with us! We don't need him! He's the one it should be! Not me—not you! Him!!

BATA: How can it be me? The Carousel and the Flying Wheel are mine! I break them down—I build them up—I make the people laugh and screaaaam! Meeee!! Baaaaataaaaaa!! My machines are the greatest things in the Carnival! Without my machines you have nothing! Nothing!!

CLOWN: No Carnival needs those stupid machines when they have Artists!

BATA: You only make the Crowd cry with your bad dancing and your awful juggling. We keep you here because we feel sorry for you!

CLOWN: That's a lie—that's a lie—that's a lie! Soon it will be fifty-six balls in a spinning rainbow above me! The orchestra will soar and the Kings and Queens will come from all over the World to see me! Me!! Not your dirty, noisy, smelly machines!

BATA: No one ever juggled fifty-six balls at the same time! Tell him it's impossible, Bella!

CLOWN: Bella knows anything is possible for an Artist. Someday Bella will jump through a burning hoop on four galloping Stallions! Someday—someday!!

BATA: You can't even juggle three balls. You can't do anything! Even Nemo said you had no talent. He never knew where to put you in the lineup!

CLOWN: Another lie! I always worked with the Trapeze Acts!

BATA: Nemo put you there because the Crowd always watched the high-wire and they didn't have to look at you!

CLOWN: Make him stop it, Bella—make him stop it!

BELLA: Show him you can juggle the balls—and he'll stop.

[*There is a long pause, as* THEY *stare at the* CLOWN. *The* CLOWN *slowly takes out his three imaginary balls and sets himself. This time he is very careful, as his arm rises and falls, rises and falls, and the balls begin to arc. Once, twice, three times—then they fall and scatter.* BELLA *laughs and* BATA *picks up the* CLOWN's *imaginary balls.*]

CLOWN: They never looked up at the high-wire! They looked at me! Meeeeee!

BATA: Give *me* the drumroll!

[BATA *sets himself to juggle the imaginary balls.*]

Louder on the drums!

BELLA: Do you see him?

[BELLA *laughs and begins to beat on an imaginary drum.*]

CLOWN: No! Stop it, Bella! He'll make a Fool of himself! He doesn't know what he's doing!

[BATA *arcs the three imaginary balls and begins to juggle them. One, two, three, four, five, six—arcing and moving in a steady pattern that he controls with ease.*]

BELLA: Bravo! Bravo for the Stupendous Baa-taaaa!
CLOWN: No! Stop him! Stop him!!
BELLA: He'll juggle fifty-six balls in no time. Bravoooo!

[*The* CLOWN *rushes at* BATA *and pushes him off balance so that the imaginary balls scatter and he runs about retrieving them.*]

CLOWN: You have no style! It's all technique—no style! You don't belong with us! You're not an Artist!!

[*The light begins to fade as* BELLA *and* BATA *move toward the terrified* CLOWN.]

BATA: It should be *you*! You!!
CLOWN: No! No! Nemo will come back! He has to come back!

[*The light is almost gone now.* BELLA *and* BATA *reach out toward the* CLOWN, *as he calls into the wind.*]

Neeeee-mooooooo. . .

[*The dim light fades into darkness and only the* CLOWN's *call is left* . . .]

ooooooooooooo . . .

[. . . *and the wind rises and fades with the lingering call* . . . *and then the silence.*]

BRUTAL MANDATE

by
CRAIG PETTIGREW

(The play was first presented at the Los Angeles Actors' Theatre's Festival of Premieres in 1982.)

Original Cast
(In Order of Appearance)

ALLARD LOWENSTEIN .... Frank Birney
DENNIS SWEENEY .... David Hunt Stafford

Directed by .... Charles Parks
Produced by .... Adam Leipzig & Diane White

Bill Bushnell, Artistic Producing Director

"There's no denying what Dennis Sweeney did. He walked out of a sleetstorm last March into the Associated Press Building on Rockefeller Plaza, took the elevator to the ninth floor, and, within twenty minutes of entering the law offices of Layton and Sherman, shot Allard Lowenstein (former Congressman from New York) dead with a Spanish pistol. Precisely what happened during those twenty minutes is unclear. . . ."

Teresa Carpenter
Village Voice

THE CHARACTERS:

Dennis Sweeney   *A 37-year-old man, probably clinically insane. He is a former pupil and associate of Allard Lowenstein.*

Allard Lowenstein   *A 51-year-old man, former Congressman from New York. In the early '60s, he had been one of Sweeney's teachers as well as predominant influence. In the mid-'60s, they were associates during the Civil Rights struggle in Mississippi.*

THE SCENE: *Allard Lowenstein's office, Rockefeller Plaza, New York City.*

THE TIME: *March 14, 1980. Approximately 4:00 PM.*

[SCENE: *A law office, modestly furnished, and efficiently messy. It should contain, among other things, a nice-sized desk, one or two chairs, piles of books, magazines, and newspapers, and a corkboard with 3x5 cards pinned to it. Written on the cards in large red block letters are states' abbreviations, e.g. FLA, CA, MASS, NY, etc. Hanging from the corkboard, its string held up by a push-pin, is a racquetball racquet. On* LOWENSTEIN'S *desk are notepads, pens, pencils, family pictures, Rolodex, desk calendar, and phone with several push-button extensions. There should also be evidence of fast-food, such as Burger King wrappers, chocolate shake container, etc.*

In the dark, LOWENSTEIN *sits in his desk chair.* SWEENEY, *offstage, begins muttering to himself, paraphrasing aspects of the script, referring to himself in the third person. As he does this, the lights slowly fade up. We then see* LOWENSTEIN *at his desk, making notes for a speech. He writes quickly; the pencil attacks the paper and each idea is conveyed with a flourish of handwriting.* LOWENSTEIN *is dressed in a long-sleeve shirt and tie. The sleeves are rolled up. His jacket is draped over his chair. There is a cheerful messiness to his appearance.*

After the lights are fully up, SWEENEY *stops mumbling. A moment later, the phone buzzes.*

LOWENSTEIN *answers the phone calmly. As he picks up the phone,* SWEENEY *appears onstage, though he is well out of key light and his head is turned away from the audience. And while* SWEENEY *is technically onstage, he is not yet in the office. He can neither hear the conversation nor see* LOWENSTEIN.

SWEENEY *is dressed in faded jeans a plaid work shirt, and a blue windbreaker. He is sopping wet, having just come out of a sleetstorm. Over his shoulder he carries a khaki backpack, the kind favored by college students.*

[NOTE: *Somewhere in the room there should be visual evidence that* LOWENSTEIN *is involved with Ted Kennedy's 1980 Presidential bid. It should be something subtle, like a bumper sticker pinned to the corkboard.*]

LOWENSTEIN: Yeah? Michael . . . Uh, which Michael . . . Oh, fine. Sure, I'll talk to him.

[LOWENSTEIN *presses another phone button and now speaks with enormous enthusiasm.*]

Michael, how the hell are ya? How's school going so far? [*Pause*] You saw your political science teacher reading the *National Review* in the student lounge? [*Pause*] Well, Bill Buckley's my friend too but that doesn't mean I help to put his supper on the table, for Chrissakes. [*Pause*] Well, of course Reagan reads the *National Review*. He usually reads it while sitting on the toilet. He has this theory: Whatever he gives out, he must take in. [*Laughs. Pause.*] I just came back from Florida with Teddy Kennedy, yes . . . Well, if the South's any indication it's going to be one helluva campaign. . . . So what's up with you? [*Pause*] Listen, before I forget, I'm scheduled to come to your school in two weeks and give a speech, answer questions. You know what you could do for me? What would really help me out a lot? If you could introduce me, and then after the speech, moderate the discussion period, sort of be my right hand man. [*Pause*] Oh, great. Also, I want you to take it upon yourself to be responsible for filling the auditorium. Shouldn't be hard, eh? Just plaster the campus with signs. You know how it's done. This will be good for you too, you know. Put your goddamned political science teacher in his place! [*Laughs*] Listen, you know what? I'm having a meeting of the minds at my house this weekend to discuss the New York primary. I want you to stop by, if you can. [*Pause*] Terrific. This Saturday night, eight-thirty. We'll have a bull session and then you and I can discuss the thing at your school. [*Pause*] I'm excited, too.

[*Another phone line buzzes*]

Hold on, Michael.

[LOWENSTEIN *presses another button. Again, he uses a much calmer voice.*]

Yeah? [*Pause*]Oh yes, send him right back. And hold my calls unless Dick Donahue checks in. Okay?

[*He returns to Michael's phone call. Again, he becomes energized.*]

Michael, I'm back. Listen, gotta run. I'm so looking forward to this Saturday. And as for this thing at your school, you might even start taking ads out in the student paper. Send me the bill on that one, okay? Great. Listen, take care. See you Saturday night. Okay. Bye-bye.

[LOWENSTEIN *hangs up the phone. He exhales nervously, as if anticipating his next visitor. After a moment,* SWEENEY *enters the office and walks up behind* LOWENSTEIN, *placing a hand on his back. He smiles broadly and comes around to where* LOWENSTEIN *can see him.*]

SWEENEY: Just let me take a look at you, man.

[*They shake hands.*]

SWEENEY: A little thin on the top, a little heavy on the bottom.
LOWENSTEIN: That mound there is muscle, Dennis.

[SWEENEY *moves to sit down. He takes the khaki bag off of his shoulder and places it beside the chair.*]

SWEENEY: Yeah? I guess so . . .
LOWENSTEIN: And you look . . . Jesus, you're sopping wet.
SWEENEY: Sleetstorm, Al. Been in it all day.
LOWENSTEIN: Well, take your coat off. Would you like a towel?
SWEENEY: [*Takes off his windbreaker and hangs it over the chair.*] No, I'm okay.

LOWENSTEIN: I can't believe it's been ten years, Dennis.
SWEENEY: Believe it, believe it.

[*Pause. They look at each other and chuckle.*]

"... that if a single man plants himself on his convictions and there abide, the huge world will come 'round to him. ..."
LOWENSTEIN: Emerson. I was on a bus with Bobby Kennedy and he scribbled that on a piece of paper.
SWEENEY: I can't tell you what a ... *shock* it is to see you too, uh, hear your voice. I expected to come back and find a parking lot where my favorite playground used to be.
LOWENSTEIN: Well?
SWEENEY: You haven't changed, man. It's goddamn wonderful.
LOWENSTEIN: Hey, are you hungry? Come on, let's get some food in here. ...
SWEENEY: [*With a sudden change of tone.*] No thanks, Al. I'm, uh, *full*.
LOWENSTEIN: [*With his hand on the phone, ready to pick up and call, discreetly withdraws his hand.*] Oh.

[*Slight pause*]

SWEENEY: You go ahead, though.
LOWENSTEIN: Nah.
SWEENEY: Still watching the weight, are ya?
LOWENSTEIN: I, uh, peruse it from time to time.
SWEENEY: I remember taking you to the airport and you would make me wrestle you in abandoned waiting rooms, just so you could keep in shape. You don't still do—
LOWENSTEIN: No, no. This is what I do now.

[LOWENSTEIN *pulls the racquet off the corkboard.* SWEENEY *quickly and inquisitively reaches up and grabs it from him.*]

SWEENEY: What is this? The latest political trend? You sure must know how to put the grip on this ...

[SWEENEY *takes a few practice swings, holding the racquet incorrectly.*]

LOWENSTEIN: You play, Dennis?
SWEENEY: Sure I play. You taught me.

[LOWENSTEIN *corrects* SWEENEY's *grip.*]

LOWENSTEIN: No, the grip goes all the way around the racquet. It's not like tennis.

[SWEENEY *tries a few swings with the new grip.*]

SWEENEY: I know what your racket is, buddy.

LOWENSTEIN: Hey, I have a court tomorrow at the Yale Club if you'd like to play.
SWEENEY: Hey! I'd love to play.
LOWENSTEIN: Good. It's a date.

[LOWENSTEIN *pencils the appointment on his desk calendar.*]

SWEENEY: Good.

[*Slight pause.* SWEENEY *reaches into a side pocket of his khaki bag and pulls out some tobacco and some rolling papers. He proceeds to hand-roll a cigarette very expertly and with great concentration.*]

Wanna smoke?
LOWENSTEIN: Tobacco?
SWEENEY: Yeah, what did you think? Oh, I gave *that* up a long time ago.
LOWENSTEIN: There's a machine down the hall . . .
SWEENEY: Out of Camels.
LOWENSTEIN: Ah. Just seems like a lot of trouble, that's all.
SWEENEY: Yes, it is. "But if it's worth the effort, then one has no choice." Right? Sound familiar?

[*Slight pause.* LOWENSTEIN *contemplates the remark.*]

LOWENSTEIN: Yes, it does.
SWEENEY: [*Laughs at the recollection.*] Introductory lecture, Stanford, 1961.
LOWENSTEIN: Jesus Christ, yes. And then you got all excited. You stood up and started stammering. You had just read *Brutal Mandate,* and you said, "Now, are we gonna be talkin' about racial oppression, or what?"
SWEENEY: And you said, "Or what."

[*They gently laugh at the memory.*]

[*Quietly*] Please, can we remember something else?
LOWENSTEIN: Do you have fond memories of Stanford?
SWEENEY: Hey. Redwoods and radicals, hippies and harlots. [*Laughs*] I still have it, by the way.
LOWENSTEIN: Have what?
SWEENEY: [*Reaches into his khaki bag and pulls out a book. He holds it up but does not give it to* LOWENSTEIN.] Your book, *Brutal Mandate.*
LOWENSTEIN: No kidding!

[LOWENSTEIN *reaches for the book but* SWEENEY, *oblivious, merely flips through the pages.*]

SWEENEY: Really torn and tattered; dog-eared like crazy. [*Puts book back into bag.*] I came across it when I was packing the other day.

LOWENSTEIN: Packing?
SWEENEY: [*Lights his cigarette.*] Yep. Movin' on. So what's happening with you?
LOWENSTEIN: Well, the campaign as you can imagine. I just came back from Florida with Teddy and I feel pretty good about things. Things are picking up and people sense that there's a movement underfoot.
SWEENEY: The polls say . . .
LOWENSTEIN: I don't really care about the polls right now. I think it's early and I think if we can get, uh, *certain people* back in the fold we well may have a goddamned chance to set things straight, or at least a little straighter than they've been. . . . And it looks as though the black vote in the South will fall our way. So . . . So we wrestle from primary to primary, airport to airport.
SWEENEY: He's the last of the Three Stooges, Al.
LOWENSTEIN: Teddy? [*Pause.*] That's an odd way to put it.
SWEENEY: Do you think he'll ever live down Chappaquiddick?
LOWENSTEIN: Goddammit, why is that seen as a *political* stumbling block. Why do people continue to—
SWEENEY: Hey, I heard a good one the other day. A reporter's talking to Kennedy, right? "Mr. Kennedy, can you tell us whether you'll be running for President or not?" And Ted says, "Gentlemen, I'll drive off that bridge when I come to it."

[SWEENEY *laughs uproariously.* LOWENSTEIN *becomes grim-faced.*]

LOWENSTEIN: Now that's not funny, Dennis.
SWEENEY: Come on, it's a scream.
LOWENSTEIN: No, it's not.
SWEENEY: Come on, Al, loosen up. It's a good joke.
LOWENSTEIN: It's an *old* joke. I've heard it before.
SWEENEY: [*Stops laughing, feels slightly embarrassed.*] Oh. [*Pauses while thinking of something to say.*] Nice office . . .
LOWENSTEIN: Not really. It's alright.
SWEENEY: So are you officially practicing law, or what?
LOWENSTEIN: Or what.

[*Again they laugh at the memory, though this time* SWEENEY's *laughter subsides quickly and he begins to gently shake his head.*]

SWEENEY: No . . . Allard. I'm not that little boy anymore.
LOWENSTEIN: I know, Dennis. [*Pause*] Have you heard from Mary?
SWEENEY: Who?
LOWENSTEIN: Mary. She's working for Carter now.
SWEENEY: Uh, I don't want to talk about her.
LOWENSTEIN: Oh. Well, she's married to Peter Bourne now . . .
SWEENEY: I *said* I don't want to talk about her. My marriage to Mary was a mistake and that's that.

LOWENSTEIN: I'm sorry. Obviously you didn't come all the way up here for me to dredge up bad memories.
SWEENEY: No, not at all.
LOWENSTEIN: So what have *you* been up to? It's been more than ten years, Dennis. The last time I saw you I was about to enter the race for Congress, uh, 1968.
SWEENEY: Which you won.
LOWENSTEIN: And no thanks to you.
SWEENEY: We were in "opposition" then.
LOWENSTEIN: We were in "opposition" long before that.

[*The phone buzzes.* LOWENSTEIN *quickly answers it.*]

Yeah? Good. Thank you.

[LOWENSTEIN *presses another button*]

LOWENSTEIN: Dick? Hi. [*Pause*] You want me to go to Buffalo? [*Pause*] Well, who do we have up there now? [*Pause*] Uh-huh. I'm with an old friend right now, Dennis Sweeney. You've heard me talk about him. [*Pause*]Yeah, a half an hour then. Fine.

[LOWENSTEIN *hangs up the phone.* SWEENEY *becomes distraught.*]

SWEENEY: Come on, a half an hour? There's so much I need to say to—
LOWENSTEIN: No, I want you to come with me. That was Dick Donahue, Ted's campaign manager in New York.
SWEENEY: I know who Dick Donahue is.
LOWENSTEIN: Good. Hey, we could get together, talk strategies again, maybe—
SWEENEY: No, Al.
LOWENSTEIN: You know what we could do, Dennis, we could—
SWEENEY: Go back to Mississippi? [*Slight pause*] No, I don't think so.
LOWENSTEIN: Just checking.
SWEENEY: *That's* it, *that's* it . . . I remember the precise moment I started to hate you, man. The Freedom Summer; the summer of '64.
LOWENSTEIN: Yes, I know. I was there.
SWEENEY: But then you left, Al. You got us down there for your Civil Rights crusade, gave us the rap, and then got in some goddamned airplane and left us to fight World War Three. Al, I went there to register people to *vote*, man. You didn't exactly tell us about the rednecks and the shotguns and the firebombs. And the blacks didn't care for us, either. "You want me to vote? You call me 'Mister.'"
LOWENSTEIN: But you became the leader, Dennis. Not Bob. Not anybody else. The Stanford newspaper ran page one stories about you every day. You became a hero.
SWEENEY: Oh yeah? I was the leader, alright. Here's how I lead: "Alright now, take cover. Hear the trucks? Billy, get over there and

stay down. I said stay down. Mary? Mary? Get away from the fucking window, honey. I said get away from the goddamned window!"

[SWEENEY *gets carried away and starts to play-act the scene.*]

"Okay, I can hear them coming." "Dennis, man, let's make a run for it." "Shut-up, Bob. Stay put. Okay now . . . Silence . . ."
LOWENSTEIN: Dennis, don't do this to yourself.
SWEENEY: "Oh my God, they've broken in. We're going to die. . . ."

[SWEENEY *inadvertently runs into* LOWENSTEIN's *arms and immediately pushes himself away.*]

LOWENSTEIN: Enough games, Dennis!
SWEENEY: Where were you, man? Our house is being firebombed and you're wrestling people in airports.
LOWENSTEIN: The truth is, Dennis, you became a leader in Mississippi because you wanted to be. It was nothing I did. It was *you* that stayed, *you* that saw it through. You saw it through because you had power, you had purpose . . . and you were in love.

[*Long pause. Again,* SWEENEY *is slightly embarrassed, unsure how to continue. He gets out of his chair and slowly walks downstage, looking out of* LOWENSTEIN's *office window. After a moment, he chuckles.*]

SWEENEY: Al?
LOWENSTEIN: Yeah?
SWEENEY: You got a shitty view.

[*They laugh.* LOWENSTEIN *comes from behind his desk and joins* SWEENEY, *putting his arm around him.*]

LOWENSTEIN: That's the great thing about New York; even if I had a great view, it would be a shitty view.

[*They laugh.*]

SWEENEY: That's true of a lot of things.

[*They start to cross from downstage right to downstage left.*]

LOWENSTEIN: I suppose. So why won't you tell me what you've been up to?
SWEENEY: Oh no, I haven't been avoiding it. It's . . . just not too interesting. I've been about . . . Doing carpentry, construction, working with my hands, going insane from time to time. The usual. You know, I was with some guys in California and we had a rock band for a little while.
LOWENSTEIN: Playing what?
SWEENEY: Oh, I *held* a guitar. I held it very well.

[*They laugh*]

LOWENSTEIN: I can't see it.
SWEENEY: You should have *heard* it, man.

[*They walk back upstage.* LOWENSTEIN *still has his arm around* SWEENEY's *shoulders.*]

LOWENSTEIN: So . . . Do you like your work?
SWEENEY: What . . . what work?
LOWENSTEIN: Your carpentry, whatever.

[*They stop walking*]

SWEENEY: Al, I don't have a pot to piss in, man.

[LOWENSTEIN *quickly pulls his wallet out.*]

LOWENSTEIN: Well Jesus, why didn't you say so at the beginning? How much do you want?
SWEENEY: No, I didn't come here to hit you up, that's not why I . . .
LOWENSTEIN: Dennis, where are you staying? Huh? I want you to come out to the house, spend some time, get to know each other again. Forget politics.
SWEENEY: No, no Al. I don't want anything from you. I came here because I wanted to see you, because I had to know . . .
LOWENSTEIN: Dennis, I'm still your friend if that's what you—

[SWEENEY *starts to break down*]

SWEENEY: No! I had to know if after all these years you were still Allard Lowenstein.
LOWENSTEIN: Of course I am.
SWEENEY: Why? I'm not Dennis Sweeney anymore. I just look like him.

[SWEENEY *collapses into* LOWENSTEIN's *arms. He is crying.*]

LOWENSTEIN: Somebody has to be us, right?
SWEENEY: It's not the same anymore.
LOWENSTEIN: Of course it's not the same, Dennis. Look at your friends from the peace movement.
SWEENEY: I don't want to talk about them.
LOWENSTEIN: Tom Hayden's married to Jane Fonda, a movie star for chrissakes . . . Jerry Rubin's a financial analyst on Wall Street. They wear suits and ties . . . They play racquetball to stay in shape . . . And politically, they're in my court now. . . .
SWEENEY: Don't tell me this.
LOWENSTEIN: Dennis, I'm just confirming what you said: "It's not the same anymore." They've changed.

[*Pause. They hold each other at arm's length.*]

SWEENEY: You never did teach me how to play racquetball, did you?

[LOWENSTEIN *chuckles*]

LOWENSTEIN: No, Dennis. They didn't even have racquetball when I was your teacher.
SWEENEY: I think I watched a couple of guys play once.
LOWENSTEIN: So I'll teach you tomorrow, if you're up to it.

[SWEENEY, *suddenly excited*]

SWEENEY: Hey, teach me now, okay?
LOWENSTEIN: Dennis, do you realize . . .
SWEENEY: Let's get a court, right now, come on.
LOWENSTEIN: That's impossible, Dennis. I have to run in a few minutes and besides you have to reserve those courts days in advance.

[*Pause.* SWEENEY, *disappointed, breaks from* LOWENSTEIN *and walks upstage right, his back turned to him.*]

Now just hold on, Dennis. We'll play tomorrow afternoon. You are still the most impetuous person I've ever known.

[*Slight pause.* SWEENEY *turns around to face* LOWENSTEIN.]

SWEENEY: When was the last time you talked to Mary?
LOWENSTEIN: [*Walks toward his desk*] I thought you didn't want to talk about her.
SWEENEY: Just curious.
LOWENSTEIN: We talk from time to time. She gives me information about Carter, we talk about old times, nothing much.
SWEENEY: She ever talk about me?
LOWENSTEIN: You know, for a long time we thought you were dead. We had no idea where you were. I tell you I was stunned when you called and made the appointment. We'd heard that you had committed suicide. Didn't sound like you at all.
SWEENEY: Al what did she say about me?
LOWENSTEIN: Nothing, Dennis. Nothing at all.
SWEENEY: Oh come on, Al.
LOWENSTEIN: [*Flips through his Rolodex. Pulls out a card and hands* SWEENEY *the phone.*] Look, here's her D.C. number. Wanna call her?
SWEENEY: No! No, forget it.

[SWEENEY *sits back down in his chair.* LOWENSTEIN *checks his watch, and then puts on his coat, as if to leave.*]

LOWENSTEIN: Why don't you come with me, Dennis?

SWEENEY: Because you're going to try and get me involved in this goddamned campaign of yours and I am not interested anymore.
LOWENSTEIN: No one gets involved unless he wants to. Or needs to.
SWEENEY: Oh, bullshit, Al. Listen, I know how you operate. If I came with you you'll start to nudge me and nudge me until I fall into some slot of yours. Now I haven't fit into a slot of yours since Mississippi, and there ain't no goddamned Kennedy going to turn me around now. Al, he's a *politician*, just like the rest of them. And you know what? They're gonna shoot him dead just like they did his brothers because . . . because it is *necessary!* Don't you see? The Triumvirate? The Holy Trinity?
LOWENSTEIN: [*Sits at his desk*] And so what do we do? Sit back and wait for Sweeney's prophecies to come true? Do we sit and let George Bush or Ronald Reagan slide into the White House and flush the continental toilet? Or do we go with a set of convictions born out of selflessness?
SWEENEY: Convictions? Al, how can you use that word? And you use it all the time, I know, because I *hear* you say it, day in and day out. Truth of the matter is, Al, you never wanted to be anything more than a slumlord in Camelot. Right?
LOWENSTEIN: Come on, Dennis, you can do better than that. You called me that in '68 when Bobby was running. I still don't know what it means.
SWEENEY: Analyze the components, Al. "A slumlord . . . in Camelot."
LOWENSTEIN: [*Rises to leave, gathering papers from his desk.*] I have to go. I'll see you tomorrow.
SWEENEY: No, come on, Al. You've got a few minutes. Hear me out. Okay? Tomorrow we'll play and forget this ever happened.

[*Slight pause.* LOWENSTEIN *drops his papers back on his desk. He walks about.*]

LOWENSTEIN: A slumlord in Camelot, huh?
SWEENEY: Yep.
LOWENSTEIN: It's not such an ignoble aspiration. Theoretically, a political structure has to have, like Camelot, an equal or greater amount of strength at the bottom as it does the top.
SWEENEY: [*Laughs.*] Man, is this the wrong decade for this conversation, or what?
LOWENSTEIN: Or what.
SWEENEY: Don't fuckin' do that to me!
LOWENSTEIN: It's a reflex, Dennis. [*Pause*] Remember when you bailed me out of jail?
SWEENEY: [*Looks away from* LOWENSTEIN] Yep.
LOWENSTEIN: You walked out of an exam when you heard, didn't you?

SWEENEY: Yep.
LOWENSTEIN: You drove 48 hours straight just to bail me out.
SWEENEY: It was the first time I had ever been to Mississippi.
LOWENSTEIN: Would you do it again?
SWEENEY: [*Looks up at* LOWENSTEIN.] You know, that's the first time I heard your voice.
LOWENSTEIN: Oh yeah?
SWEENEY: Driving to Mississippi. You kept talking to me.
LOWENSTEIN: Could have been a liberal radio station.
SWEENEY: You were saying the same stuff you say now, having all the answers. Like I would ask a question; "Should I do this, or what?" And your voice would always say, "Or what."
LOWENSTEIN: Dennis, I've always found it funny. It stems from when I was your teacher.
SWEENEY: Yes, but it's not the same anymore!

[*Pause.* LOWENSTEIN *gathers some papers from his desk and prepares to leave.*]

LOWENSTEIN: Come on, let's go. [*Starts to exit.*]
SWEENEY: "Take it upon yourself to fulfill another person's good intentions."
LOWENSTEIN: [*Laughs, mostly out of frustration.*] What in the hell is that?
SWEENEY: Something you said once; something I still hear.
LOWENSTEIN: Jesus, I must have been young.
SWEENEY: It was in Mississippi. You were my age then.
LOWENSTEIN: Sounds like it.
SWEENEY: And then you left us alone.

[*Pause.* LOWENSTEIN *nervously checks his watch and starts to leave.*]

LOWENSTEIN: Look, we've done this already, Dennis. Get your coat. I'm late as it is.
SWEENEY: Allard, I want the voices to stop.

[*Slight pause.*]

LOWENSTEIN: What, Dennis?
SWEENEY: Let's be upfront, Al. If you've talked to Mary, then you know what's going on here, because *I* have talked to Mary.
LOWENSTEIN: [*Comes back to his desk, puts his papers down. Picks up phone.*] Let me call Dick.
SWEENEY: [*Quickly rises and hangs up the phone.*] Oh no, don't call anybody.
LOWENSTEIN: [*Gently pushes* SWEENEY's *hand away.*] I know what you're talking about, Dennis. Just let me . . .

SWEENEY: Where were you, man? Our house is being firebombed and you're wrestling people in airports.

SWEENEY: [*Pulls the phone cord out of the floor.*] No! I want the *voices* to stop!
LOWENSTEIN: I'm trying to help you! You either want my help or you don't want my help. Which is it?
SWEENEY: I want the voices to stop!
LOWENSTEIN: Okay. Listen, Mary told me . . .
SWEENEY: What did Mary tell you?
LOWENSTEIN: Mary told me about the voices. You had called her to tell her that Allard Lowenstein had planted voices in your head, and to tell him to turn them off.
SWEENEY: [*In a quiet rage, which grows into an anguished plea.*] Turn them off? Turn them off? That's not how Mary put it, is it? No, that sounds more like one of your expressions. Just like the people in your life. You turn them on, and when they grow up different than your blueprint, you turn them off. Probably got some college kid in tow even as we speak, referring to him as your protegé, no, your "right hand man." But you're not a good duck, Mallard. A good duck will look back at her ducklings and love all of them, no matter how ugly one of them may turn out to be. And I turned out to be one of the ugliest ducklings you ever spawned. And you couldn't accept that. So before I swam away from the fold, you planted your voice inside my head, to make sure you had your hook in me forever . . . I've been trying to get rid of your voice for the last ten years. . . . First, you had your dentist-friend in Mississippi put a radio receiver in the back of my mouth. Well, I took the pliers and I ripped the bridgework clean out, clean out. I had evil coming through my teeth, Allard. Evil through my teeth from the voices in my brain. You were telling me to kill myself, over and over, like a continual tape loop. And then one night, when I was sleeping, you came in and planted an electrode in my brain. I went to Paris to see a brain surgeon. He wouldn't operate. He wouldn't remove the voices from my head. They said . . . They said I was . . . They said I was . . .

[SWEENEY *breaks down. He sits back in the chair and buries his face in his hands, sobbing.*]

But it's not my fault, it's not my fault. Help me! Help me stop the voices that control my mind so I can go home again.

[*Pause.* SWEENEY *weeps.* LOWENSTEIN *comes over and stands behind* SWEENEY, *putting his hands on his shoulders. After a moment,* LOWENSTEIN *leans over and speaks directly into* SWEENEY's *ear.*]

LOWENSTEIN: We'll stop the voices. . . .

[*Pause.* LOWENSTEIN *moves back and sits behind his desk.* SWEENEY's *weeping subsides. While at his desk,* LOWENSTEIN *flips through his Rolodex and starts writing an address and phone number on a piece of scratch paper.*]

Dennis, I want you to see this guy.
SWEENEY: [*Raises his head out of his hands.*] What?
LOWENSTEIN: A friend of mine. Have him send me the bill. He'll be in his office for another hour. Please.
SWEENEY: [*Slowly rises and goes to stand next to the desk.*] Will he stop the voices?
LOWENSTEIN: I think so.
SWEENEY: Is he a brain surgeon?
LOWENSTEIN: He's a doctor.
SWEENEY: Shrink?
LOWENSTEIN: He's a doctor. A friend of mine.

[SWEENEY *takes the piece of paper from* LOWENSTEIN. SWEENEY'S *mood changes. He seems more confident.*]

SWEENEY: Okay. [*Puts on his jacket and hangs the khaki bag over his shoulder.*]
LOWENSTEIN: You're one tough sonofabitch to figure out, you know that?
SWEENEY: Yeah. Guess so.

[SWEENEY *starts to exit.* LOWENSTEIN *rises to embrace him.*]

LOWENSTEIN: I'm glad you came, Dennis. You know, when Mary told me about this I wanted to help you somehow. I hope we can straighten this out together.
SWEENEY: [*Gently breaks the embrace.*] Don't, Al. I'm . . . I'm gonna go. I'll see you tomorrow. [*He starts to exit.*]
LOWENSTEIN: Call me tonight if you want to. My home phone is on the back.
SWEENEY: [*Looks at the other side of the piece of paper.*] Yeah. I'll do that.
LOWENSTEIN: [*Pantomiming a racquetball swing.*] Around two o'clock tomorrow, if you want to.
SWEENEY: See you then.

[SWEENEY *exits and stops at the edge of the light, his back to* LOWENSTEIN, *where he emerged at the beginning of the play. He stands there, motionless, for a couple of beats.* LOWENSTEIN *starts fiddling with the ripped-out telephone cord.* SWEENEY *then quickly re-enters.*]

Uh, did you call me, Al?
LOWENSTEIN: No, no, I didn't.
SWEENEY: Could've sworn I heard you call me.

LOWENSTEIN: Nope.

[*Pause. They look at each other and chuckle at the confusion.*]

SWEENEY: Well . . .

[*Slight pause*]

LOWENSTEIN: Just wondering how to explain this to the phone company.
SWEENEY: [*Laughs. He seems almost like a friendly little boy.*] Man, was I crazy to do that, or what?
LOWENSTEIN: [*casually, without thinking*] Or what.

[*Slight pause.* LOWENSTEIN *has unwittingly detonated the bomb inside* SWEENEY.]

SWEENEY: That's it. Get behind your desk.

[SWEENEY *crosses downstage.*]

LOWENSTEIN: Dennis, I was kidding. Now go see my friend before he leaves for the day.
SWEENEY: Just shut up!

[SWEENEY *pulls a gun out of his khaki bag. After he pulls the gun out, he drops the bag to the floor. He takes the gun and, rather than pointing it at* LOWENSTEIN, *he puts it to his own temple.* LOWENSTEIN *becomes frantic, but stays behind his desk.*]

LOWENSTEIN: Jesus, Dennis, don't be stupid. Give me the gun!
SWEENEY: No, Al. It's the only way to stop the circus. [*Places the gun barrel inside his mouth.*] "Take it upon yourself to fulfill another person's good intentions."

[SWEENEY *grows very intense. His head shakes as he is about to pull the trigger.*]

LOWENSTEIN: Dennis, that's not my intention at all. By destroying yourself, you silence *your* voice, not the voices in your head.

[SWEENEY *relaxes a bit, and* LOWENSTEIN *moves from behind his desk. As soon as* LOWENSTEIN *moves,* SWEENEY *grows intense again, shoving the gun into one of his eyes. After a tense beat,* LOWENSTEIN *breaks from behind his desk and rushes* SWEENEY.]

LOWENSTEIN: Dear God, Dennis! Give me the gun!
SWEENEY: NO!

[SWEENEY *yanks the gun away from his eye and shoots* LOWENSTEIN *twice, who instantly falls to the floor, still writhing.* SWEENEY *walks upstage, around the desk, and shoots* LOWENSTEIN *four more times.* LOWENSTEIN *is silenced.* SWEENEY *stands at his shooting position for several moments, surrounded by the gun's smoke. He sees the cloud surrounding him and begins to inhale the smoke with a perverse satisfaction. He holds the warm gun to his cheek. He then comes over to* LOWENSTEIN, *bends down to touch him, but stops short of making physical contact. He stands back up and looks down at* LOWENSTEIN.]

SWEENEY: Dead . . . [*After a moment, places the gun on the desk and sits in* LOWENSTEIN'*s chair. He looks around. What was once an eerie smile now turns into a look of perplexity.*]

Is he dead? Or what?

[*Lights fade to black.*]

THEY WON'T LET ME PAY YOUR RENT, JACK!

by
ALAN ORMSBY

(The play was first presented at the Los Angeles Actors' Theatre's Playwrights' Workshop Festival of One-Acts in 1978.)

Original Cast
(In Order of Appearance)

HOWARD .... Burr DeBenning
JACK .... Pierrino Mascarino

Directed by .... Alan Ormsby
Produced by .... Diane White

Ralph Waite, Artistic Director

They Won't Let Me Pay Your Rent, Jack!

[SCENE: *A small musty room, one door, one window. Five locks on the door, of various kinds, including a police lock. The window is small, has bars, and overlooks a gray courtyard. The light that shines through this window does so at an oblique angle, stretching the shadow of the bars across the U.S. wall. Against the wall, two cots. Between them, on a night stand, a large wind-up clock. Center, a solitary suspended light bulb in a paper shade. Left, an old-fashioned gas stove and a small refrigerator. On the refrigerator door a large flashlight. D.L. a bathroom, no door, instead a blanket suspended by clothespins. Right, a small card table covered with books, papers, tensor lamp, small manual typewriter, vintage model. An upended wooden crate, capped with small pillow, serves as chair for this table.*

HOWARD, *pale, thin, irritable, sits at typewriter, waiting.*
JACK, *large, healthy, powerfully built, stands U.S. waiting.*
Pause. HOWARD *begins to type, slowly at first.* JACK *smiles.*
HOWARD's *typing grows faster as he gets involved in the work.*
JACK *starts to sing in a choppy sing-songy rhythm, beginning as a whisper, adding volume as he goes along.*]

JACK: 'Do—you—know—the—way—to—San—Jo—se? I'm—goin'—back—to—find—(etc.)

[*Instantly* HOWARD's *typing falls into the song's rhythm. He stops writing, stares at typewriter.*]

HOWARD: Jack —

[JACK *stops singing, covers his mouth, suppresses giggle.* HOWARD *sighs, rubs the back of his neck, after a pause begins typing again.* JACK *again starts to sing, in same rhythm as before*]

JACK: 'L—A—is—a—great—big—free—way—Put—a hun-dred—down—and—buy—a—car—'
HOWARD: Jack —
JACK: Why don't you like her —
HOWARD: Why don't I like her —
JACK: You're my friend —
HOWARD: I'm your friend —
JACK: It's important that you like her —
HOWARD: Why are you so interested Jack what's the difference whether or not I like her YOU like her why do YOU like her Jack why are YOU so interested — She tells you no no NO a thousand times NO she doesn't ever want to hear see smell have ANYTHING to do with you ever again and — STILL you're interested and TELLING me TELLING me all the time about her weeks Jack MONTHS

telling me how interested YOU are in her but she DOESN'T INTEREST ME, Jack She DOESN'T INTEREST ME man I don't DISLIKE her I don't LIKE her I don't CARE —

JACK: We have a deal — it's IMPORTANT that you like her —

HOWARD: Our deal says that I write and that you pay the rent our deal says nothing about me liking her, her liking me, me liking you, you liking her, us liking each other or ourselves; if our deal had related to her, me or you in any personal way shape or form whatsoever, we would not have had a deal to begin with —

JACK: [Pleadingly] I WANT you to like her —

HOWARD: Our deal says nothing about what you want or what I want; our deal assigns us functions and those functions we shall fulfill as long as breath keeps us running the hyphen between our dates of birth and death —

JACK: I love her —

HOWARD: Good for you, Jack, good for you, you love her, GOOD FOR YOU —

JACK: I LOVE HER!!

HOWARD: Go away, Jack.

JACK: We're going to get married—we're getting married and going to Bimini for our honeymoon—there's a hotel there, we're going to get married and stay at this hotel for our honeymoon—I'm going to work as a bartender, she'll see me shaking up the cocktails in my white jacket and my black pants, shake shake shake—she'll see me shaking up the cocktails, she'll be sitting at a little white metal table, a little, white, wrought-iron table, and I'll smile, she'll smile back and wave her hand like this and the marimba band will be playing "Melody D'Amour" and "Yellow Bird" and "Do You Know The Way to San Jose?"—I like "Yellow Bird", I like "Do You Know The Way to San Jose?" — [sings] 'Do—you—know—the—way—to—'

HOWARD: Please don't sing, Jack.

JACK: 'San—Jo-se—I'm—go—ing—back—to—'

HOWARD: It's not polite to sing in a room with just one window; the lyrics get stuck; they get caught; they can't get out; they go to your head, Jack, they whirlpool around in there, they get into the bloodstream and they come out through your fingers when you write things and San Jose keeps appearing in your stories, stories which take place in Europe in the eighteenth-century and have nothing to do with California —

JACK: We'll send you Xmas cards every Xmas from Bimini and you'll come down for a vacation to see us, Howard, to see the sun, the sand, the sea, the stars, the stars, the sea, the sand, the sun — [HOWARD grits his teeth and goes back to typing] We'll have three kids then, me and her, two boys and a GIRL, no, make that two girls and a BOY, Sandy, Kenny and Douglas, I mean Sandy, JENNY and Douglas— Douglas has a case of fungus on his scalp right here so he has to wear an aviator cap from Army-Navy Surplus on his head so he can't pick at the fungus while it heals —

[HOWARD *stops typing, stares in horror at what he just wrote.*]

HOWARD: Douglas is in my story, Jack —

JACK: Running down the beach, all three, sand on her brown back, 'will you scratch me there, Daddy?' — rubbing away the sand on her brown back, my big hand, I can put it on the top of her head, my hand covers the top of her head —

HOWARD: [*Pulling paper from machine*] Douglas is in my story, Jack, and the other little bastards too, right there in eighteenth-century France, Jack, right there in his aviator's cap — [*He crumples the paper and throws it on the floor*]

JACK: Up to Mommy on the terrace, over the rail, running the length of the big blue pool, there's Mommy, Oh! I smile, I smile, and she'll smile back and wave her hand like this and turn her head like this and lean her chin on her hand and her teeth will look wet, oh they'll glisten with wet almost slimy with wet the way wet teeth do when the lips open up and they smile out from under the shadow of her big straw hat, huge and floppy like a manta ray —

HOWARD: OH GOD JACK PLEASE!!

JACK: HI MOMMY! HI SANDY! HI JENNY! HI DOUGLAS! Smiling at them, so happy and tears in her eyes under the big straw hat and reaching out to me with her hand and holding hands under the table, I love this part of her, here — [JACK *touches the side of his body just below the rib cage*] when she lies on her side, on the beach, or in our bed, the way her body dips and then goes up, plus I love her neck, the way it holds up her head, and her head —

HOWARD: Jack, a little treacle may do in a pinch, but not as a CONSTANT DIET, Jack, NOT EVERY DAY, Jack, NOT FOREVER!

JACK: — and her eyes and her voice and her life — I love her life most of all Howard, the way she moves in it —

HOWARD: Yeah, we know how she moves in it —

JACK: Don't, Howard.

HOWARD: Up and down she moves in it, all night long.

JACK: I said DON'T.

HOWARD: Admit it, Jack, you love a hooker!

JACK: LIAR!

HOWARD: Shall I prove it to you, Jack? Wanna put it to the test?

JACK: You spoil things.

HOWARD: Give me the money, I'll call her up —

JACK: Leave her alone —
HOWARD: Twenty-five bucks, come on I'll call her —
JACK: I know her, I love her —
HOWARD: That's your problem, not mine, don't punish me because you love a hooker —
JACK: LIAR!
HOWARD: Prove it! Prove I'm wrong, Jack.

[JACK *goes to table, takes out money, comes back, slams it down on the table*]

JACK: Liar! Double liar!

[HOWARD *gets up calmly, takes money, puts on coat, goes to door, unlocks each lock slowly, occasionally glancing at* JACK, *opens the door.*]

JACK: Don't call her, don't call her—I love her, she loves me—

[HOWARD *closes door, comes back to* JACK; *firmly:*]

HOWARD: Don't ever sing near me again. NEVER AGAIN.

[JACK *lowers his head.* HOWARD *smiles triumphantly, takes off coat, sits back down at typewriter, begins to work. Three beats.*]

JACK: [*Softly*] Hi, Mommy—Shake, shake, shake—[*Giggles*] Strawberry daiquiri—banana daiquiri—[*Like a child*] 'Do you—know—the—way—to—'

[HOWARD *stops writing.* JACK *stops singing.* HOWARD *resumes typing*]

JACK: [*Still whispering*]. 'San—Jo-se—I'm—go—in'—back—to—find—[*Growing louder*]—some—peace—of—mind—in—'

[HOWARD *stops typing, slams hands down on table, rises, pushing carton over, goes to table, takes money, goes to door, takes coat, opens door, looks back at* JACK]

HOWARD: Okay, Jack. Just okay.

[*He exits.* JACK *stares at door. Lights fade.*]

Scene ii

[HOWARD *in socks and underwear is packing a suitcase. Off, the sound of footsteps.* HOWARD *freezes. Footsteps pass. With urgency, he begins packing up his papers, writing materials, etc. then starts to put on pants when the door bursts open and* JACK, *tears streaming down his face, blood on his hands and shirt, enters. He slams door, leans against it, crying, staring at* HOWARD]

HOWARD: Take it easy, Jack—
JACK: Yuh! Tuh! Muh!—[*He can't speak; shakes his head violently*] Yuh! Tuh! Muh! Muh!
HOWARD: I told you about her didn't I tell you about her? You have to admit I told you—

[JACK *picks up chair, holds it above his head*]

HOWARD: I'm your friend, Jack, I'M YOUR FRIEND!
JACK: Yuh! Tuh! Muh! [*Clearly in pain,* JACK *puts the chair down and sits in it, staring at* HOWARD]
HOWARD: Okay. I can see it's time for me to go. All right, Jack, I'll leave. I'll just—go.
[HOWARD *continues dressing, packing, as he talks*] I'll just—move out. I'm sorry, but I'd say—for both of us—the deal has become—uh—non-progressional—I think you'll agree, once you—once you regain—ah—the verbal facility—
[HOWARD *picks up suitcase, starts out*]

HOWARD: I'm just—going to—go now—[*He moves toward door;* JACK *grabs him by the throat*] Jack—what—what're you—doing—

[JACK *takes keys from* HOWARD's *pocket; goes to door and begins locking locks one by one*]

HOWARD: Oh boy. Gonna make it bad for me, huh Jack? Gonna do your best, right? Come on. Let me out, Jack. Don't be silly.

[JACK *takes keys off chain and swallows them one by one. Lights fade.*]

Scene iii

[*A flashlight goes on. The beam travels the room, stops on* HOWARD's *bed: Empty. The beam travels around, moving faster and faster, then stops. The overhead bulb goes on.* JACK, *holding flashlight, stands looking for* HOWARD, *who is gone.* JACK *checks door and window, then goes to* HOWARD's *bed and moves it aside.* HOWARD *lies on the floor, hands folded in attitude of cadaver.*]

HOWARD: Mm—yes, fine, comfortable— mm-hum— what'll happen eventually—now that my, um, 'associate' has quit his job—is that, after we don't pay the bills for a while they'll shut off the lights and the gas and then evict us — 'An unpaid bill can break any lock they make' — family aphorism. So—it's just—FINE.

[JACK *turns off light. Sound of clock. Suddenly flashlight goes on, like spotlight, on* HOWARD's *face, simultaneously* JACK *screams.*]

HOWARD: Cut it out Jack, CUT IT OUT, cut out that goddamn screaming it's not worth it, not for that WHORE, not for that BITCH, not for that GODDAMN HOOKER, cut it out!

[*Flashlight off;* JACK's *scream ends simultaneously.*]

Scene iv

[JACK *at refrigerator;* HOWARD *seated*]

HOWARD: Really, I don't care about it. I'm not even hungry. I just looked in there to, you know, keep count. Actually the less you eat the less appetite you have, stock observation, probably true. No, no, no, really, I don't want anything, thanks anyway.

[JACK *takes food from refrigerator, throws it out window.*]

Uh-hunh. Okay. Good. You missed the cereal.

[JACK *takes cereal, throws it out, too*]

You're incredible, Jack — [*Laughs*] — really incredible. It's funny, Jack, don't you see it's funny? [*Laughs*] Funny —

[*Lights fade*]

Scene v

[*Moonlight reveals* JACK *asleep in chair by the door.* HOWARD *watches him from across the room. He opens a drawer, takes out a knife. Crosses toward* JACK. *Raises knife over* JACK's *heart. Tries to bring it down. Can't. Crosses to table. Takes out joint. Lights it from stove. Tokes. Blows smoke out window. Light goes on,* HOWARD *turns to see* JACK, *awake and watching him.*]

HOWARD: Oh, hi. I was just going to wake you.

[*He offers the joint.* JACK *snatches it away, tosses it out the window.*]

Good aim, Jack. Like that aim.

[JACK *goes to table, finds the knife and leftover ounce of dope*]

Tell you what: Trade you the knife for the dope, one narcotic for the other, whattaya say?

[JACK *puts the dope in the oven*]

They Won't Let Me Pay Your Rent, Jack!

You're pissing me off royally, you know that, Jack? I mean you can pretend there's some, you know, BIG MORAL DILEMMA here all you want, but there's no MORAL DILEMMA here at all, the only thing keeping me from freedom is your physical dominance.

[JACK *gets typewriter, puts it in oven*]

My favorite aunt gave me that typewriter. She also sold me the dope. Joke, Jack? Haha? I can laugh too, see, I can still laugh. HAHAHAHA! Look: Why not burn the manuscript, too? Here, go ahead —

[*Begins piling up the reams of typed manuscript*]

Sure — 'cause I screwed your hooker? It's an even trade—Go ahead — Ten years' work, no carbons, it'll burn quick — be my guest —

[JACK *carries papers tauntingly to stove*]

Just remember that Douglas is in it, Jack, and the marimba band and the hotel in Bimini—all worked into the fiber of life in eighteenth-century France — it works! Kind of — ironical historical juxtapositions — kind of — Doctorow-like! Interesting! Kind of K-Mart and Versailles! GOOD MOVIE! Go ahead, burn it, enjoy! It'll be fun watching Douglas burn up in his aviator's cap, trying to bail out — it'll be fun watching the marimba band go up in smoke, smiling — might improve their playing, who knows? — Think their smiles are wet enough, slimy enough to put the fire out, Jack? Go ahead, burn it, it's my last request —

[JACK *lowers his head as though weeping*]

Not so funny now, hunh, Jack?

[JACK *looks up; He is laughing. He puts the manuscript in the oven, slams the door, laughs loud and hard.* HOWARD *shrugs; pretends indifference; crosses to desk, starts to speak; can't; suddenly covers his face, tries to stifle a racking sob. Lights out.*]

Scene vi

[HOWARD *alone, pacing*]

HOWARD: No way, the answer is no, I will tell you nothing, Jack, nothing, not one FUCKING THING! You want details? You want confession? You want to dwell on this thing with this kind of morbid intensity that's your problem, Jack, not mine! YOU'RE NOT GETTING ANYTHING OUTTA ME!

[JACK *groans from bathroom*]

Well, I—I guess you thought it would be EASY digesting five doorkeys! Maybe you thought it would UNLOCK the 'REAL' YOU, right, Jack? Uh-hunh, uh-hunh, the 'Real' Jack —

[JACK *goans, offstage;* HOWARD *calls to him*]

JACK OF HEARTS, right Jack? Haha! — Jack of HEARTS, CLUBS, SPADES, DIAMONDS — but not quite a full deck, right Jack? JACK ARMSTRONG! JACK THE JAILER! Getting warm here, getting closer to the 'real' Jack, right Jack? NEANDERTHAL JACK! Like it, like it — BIG JACK! Big BAD Jack! Big Bad MEAN Jack! JACK OFF! JACK ON! You like that, Jack? The polarities? Oh, but wait—oh hey, this is IT, Jack —

[*Calling into bathroom*]

JACK THE RIPPER!

[JACK *stumbles on from bathroom, runs to bed, falls down across it*]

JACK THE RIPPER! Knew it, knew it, the hit dog always hollers! So am I right, Jack? Blink twice for yes, once for no — I'm right, aren't I Ripper?
JACK: Yuh—Kah—Muh —
HOWARD: It's okay! I don't want your confession! If you killed her okay, fine, IT HAS NOTHING TO DO WITH ME AND I DON'T WANT THE DETAILS! Anyway, these things are universal, Jack, sex and murder are events our imaginations explore on their own, without benefit of exact description! Facts disappoint! Imagination feeds on inference! sometimes to the point of obesity! But will an exchange of graphic, perhaps PORNOGRAPHIC confessions between us serve to reduce the bloat?

[*His stomach growls*]

Hunger prompts these metaphors. No—you don't tell me what you did with her and I won't tell you what I did with her and we'll both be better off. IN FACT I REFUSE TO TELL YOU ANY GODDAMN THING AT ALL!

[*He sits in chair by the door looking at Jack*]

JACK: Uh! Kah! Ahh —
HOWARD: I SAID NO DON'T TELL ME!

[JACK *makes stabbing motions with his hands*]

AND DON'T SHOW ME, EITHER!

[*He turns his chair around so that he is facing the door. Pause. Then* JACK

They Won't Let Me Pay Your Rent, Jack! 95

begins to hum — grotesquely — 'Do You Know the Way to San Jose.' Enraged, HOWARD *stands, faces him.*]

HOWARD: Okay, buster, you want it? You really want it? OKAY, GODDAMMIT, THEN YOU'RE GONNA GET IT!

[*Pause; he gathers his thoughts*]

First she—no, wait— First I—first I took off my shirt, then she took off her dress—folded it— wait— I folded it— no, no, wait—SHE folded it— Wait—FIRST— Okay, the cab, she came in a cab, not CAME in the cab I mean ARRIVED in a cab — Okay; okay; ARRIVAL. Perfunctory conversation; key in door; light on; blah, blah, okay, we're in the room— THAT'S when she took off her—No, not yet— First I paid her— she turned the bills all right-side up, folded them, put them in her purse—THEN she took off her skirt—tight and purple, color of eggplant — I turned on the radio — YOU OKAY, JACK? EVERYTHING OKAY OVER THERE? [JACK *stares at him*] Just checking, Jack! Where was I — ? It's not easy, Jack, believe me, sorting through these verbal snapshots—Oh yeah! Me unlacing my shoes, her standing there—there! pushing up and away a reluctant turtleneck that masked her face and clung to her hair like a bat—watching her body, arms upraised, black bra, cotton undies, cheap stuff up to here—little ducks and bunnies—Tell me I said to her, about Bimini—ironic, with my smile, you know— She said: HUNH? — furrowed brow, cynical grin, impatient eyes behind her horn-rimmed glasses—STOP ME IF I'M GOING TOO FAST, JACK! —Tell me, I said to her, about the white metal tables, the floppy hat, the marimba band — She said: 'Here's the party. Twenty-five bucks buys you fifteen minutes. Come by then or we start on overtime. Twenty-five bucks buys you half-and-half, a little French, a little standard, nothing kinky, I don't do Greek!' 'No Greek?' I said. 'No homage to the dawning of the Western Era?' So, so! Standard ablutions at the sink, then crossed here, all dry, sat on the edge of the bed. I lay back, expectant, she advanced, determined—she started—she stopped—she reached over and turned the clockface toward us— 'letting it watch' I thought, with its little round vicious judgmental face spitting its sibilant ticks — [*Pause*] —Splash of hair across my thighs, rhythmic bobbing of head, spot of popped light in lens of glasses, ticking of goddamned clock, and looking, looking down at that lumped gobbling form across my knees—splotches, blotches, pores, pits, marbled thighs and cellulite hips—dyed hair, shitdark at the roots—a pimple here, one there, a boo in her nose, a stain in her pants, double-bill of sweat and perfume, upper lip grim with smudge of moustache, forehead squeezing sweat — 'my mistress, when she walks, treads on the *ground*!' OF

COURSE I felt the need to transform her too, Jack, from frog to — SOMETHING! I feel that need with all experience! But not those starved and sunned survivors dodging capture in the beached recesses of the brain—not BIMINI, Jack! No, No, I said, let her be real and TAKE THE GODDAMNED CONSEQUENCES! And then she rose, one eye on the clock—'Halftime?' I said. She didn't smile.

[JACK covers his ears and groans. HOWARD grabs JACK's hands and pulls them away from his ears.]

HOWARD: OH NO! YOU WANTED TO HEAR IT NOW GET THOSE HANDS FROM YOUR EARS!

[They struggle briefly. JACK exhausted, lies back, hands at his sides.]

She rose, as I said, one eye on the clock, and wiggled up my legs and sat and rocked and waited for me and plucked at her tongue with two fingers and shook back her hair and watched the clock as she rocked up and down and in and out and up and down and in and out—the procreational moves were designed to be grasped by all mentalities — And watching her bored face, Jack, I began to see why you loved her, for she must have transformed you, as I saw she had me, from FROG to SOMETHING ELSE — In my case, MONEY, I would say—this week's groceries, this week's light bill, this week's rent— And you, Jack, you with your domestic drive would no doubt revel in the magic of such solid transformations! And in and out and up and down and OVER AND OUT! With a full three minutes to spare. EPILOGUE: Sound of shoebuckles, zippers, some casual glances — opening of door—exchange of non sequiturs—closing of door—footsteps fading down the hall— [Pause] So. Got what you wanted, Jack?

[JACK sits up, starts to speak, falls back on bed]

Jack?

[He goes to JACK, shakes him; JACK is limp]

Jack?

[He rolls JACK from side to side; no response]

Hey, come on! Wake up! Are you kidding me? WAKE UP, SHITHEAD, WAKE UP!

[He shakes JACK again, listens for heartbeat, backs away]

Oh. I see. [Pause] Okay, dead. Is that it? Okay, Jack.

[He makes 'OK' signal with thumb and forefinger]

Dead. I get it.

THEY WON'T LET ME PAY YOUR RENT, JACK!   97

[*There is suddenly a loud pounding on the door*]

WOMAN'S VOICE: [*Offstage*] Hey, Jack!

[HOWARD *looks frantically at* JACK, *then back at the door. More pounding.*]

WOMAN'S VOICE: Jack, you in there?
HOWARD: Yeah!
WOMAN'S VOICE: Where's the rent?
HOWARD: Tomorrow!
WOMAN'S VOICE: [*Suspiciously*] What?
HOWARD: [*Muffling his voice*] Tomorrow, I'll pay the rent tomorrow!
WOMAN'S VOICE: Jack pays the rent—not YOU!
HOWARD: Tomorrow, I promise —
WOMAN'S VOICE: No rent, no lights!
HOWARD: Tomorrow, please!
WOMAN'S VOICE: Not you!
HOWARD: Please!
WOMAN'S VOICE: [*Trailing off*] Not you—Jack pays the rent—not you—
HOWARD: They won't let me pay the rent, Jack. I can't leave, I can't stay — they won't let me pay the rent —

[*The overhead light sputters and starts to fade.* HOWARD *reaches out as if to catch the light. Blackout.*]

Scene vii

[*Darkness. The flashlight is turned on. The beam travels the walls, then drops suddenly to illuminate* JACK's *dead face.*]

HOWARD: Gotcha!

[*The beam rises, travels back around the room, zooming round and round and coming back to* JACK's *face*]

HOWARD: Gotcha!

[*The beam moves again, traveling more and more wildly around the room, dropping on* JACKs *dead face*]

HOWARD: Gotcha!!

[*The beam goes off. In the dark* HOWARD *laughs. Then talks calmly:*]

    Okay, Jack — let's talk about compromise. But not Bimini. La Jolla maybe—Puerto Vallarta—Paris—something I can live with.

[*The bulb fades up to about one-third intensity*]

Thank you Jack. Paris then? Give me Paris and I'll give you the — truth. I've conceded everything else.

[*He puts on a pair of sunglasses, turns back and faces the light as he makes his way weakly to sit at the table*]

Anyway, SHE wants Paris — [*Sits*] —wants to wear the powdered wigs at court, to paint the mole on the rise of her breast, to mask her face with those delicate fans and peer over them at the King—Yes, she's—she's very decent, Jack, and complex, the perfect subject for a story, not at all what I said — She's promised to let me be her ghost, 'The Memoirs', Jack, 'The Life and Times' —[*Listens*] Mm? Yes, very pleased. In fact, she's all I can think of, all I can see, I'm all clogged up with her voice—eyes—face—hair—not face-hair as in 'facial hair', but FACE. HAIR. Two separate and distinct—Yes, she told me about the hotel, but that was *then*, Jack, this is *now* —

[*As if addressing a waiter.*]

I'll have the vichyssoise—[*To* JACK] Now she comes in the window at night, she floats between the bars and fills the room, Jack, singing a capella— [*Again to 'Waiter'*]—Roquefort is fine— [*To* JACK] Paris then. But not three children. Two. Boy and girl. Or one—a combination. There's always room for humor, Jack. [*To 'Waiter'*] The veal. [*To* JACK] Oh, all right, Jack, but not if he wears his aviator cap. What? No, no, thanks all the same, His Majesty provides his own musicians— We'll miss you too, Jack, it's thanks to you I've lost my irony— And it's thanks to you I've gained my love—

[*The light sputters and starts a slow fade to black. As it fades,* HOWARD *sings softly to himself.*]

'Plaisir d'amour —
Ne dure qu'an moment—
Chagrin d'amour—
Dure toute—
La vie . . .'

[*He continues humming as the lights fade to Black*]

PROWLERS

by
PAUL MINX

(The play was first presented at the Los Angeles Actors' Theatre's Festival of Premieres in 1980.)

Original Cast
(In Order of Appearance)

WILLIE	Charles Parks
BEA	Toni Sawyer
DOLORES	Kerry Shear

Directed by .... George Loros
Produced by .... Diane White & Adam Leipzig

Bill Bushnell, Artistic Producing Director

[*The suggestion of a surburban kitchen in a state of decay—peeling wallpaper, sink full of dirty dishes, mismatched kitchen table chairs. A door leads to the basement. In the center of the room is a kitchen table covered with a cloth. There are two imaginary windows in the "fourth wall."* WILLIE, *20, a neatly dressed college student, sits at the table, methodically oiling a rifle.* BEA, *his mother, speaks off-stage.*]

BEA: [*Reading, working on phrasing.*] Your face orbiting among the dead/ waiting to be born again/as a weasel or a rat.
WILLIE: [*Looking up, mumbling.*] Born again!
BEA: "As a weasel or a rat." Do you like the poem, Willie? It's called "Lonely Nights on Earth."
WILLIE: [*Looking up, mumbling.*] Lonely nights! Poetry!
BEA: A poem! You do understand it's a poem! I'm working again, Willie. I don't want my ideas to float away like balloons in cartoon strips. Especially in this time of crisis. I mustn't forget about the arts, Willie. That's why you're home. You can worry about the practical things. You're good at that.
WILLIE: [*Calling, surly.*] Who's the rat in the poem? Is it me?
BEA: It's our father. Our ex. You remember your father, don't you? His death has been positively inspirational.
WILLIE: Was he the tall man who took out the garbage?
BEA: Handed out your allowance. Always in quarters. A methodical man. [*She searches for the words.*] I think of you . . . snarling/in the bushes at night/trying to . . . get in/to rejoin me in this warm bed.

[BEA, *a woman in her late forties, enters mid-sentence, carrying a sheaf of papers. Her hair is dishevelled. She wears a dirty bathrobe, a pencil behind her ear.*]

Your small fur-covered body/pressed smooth against . . . my side. [*PAUSE*] It needs an ending. Something to give it a little . . . so it makes sense. [*PAUSE*] How would you end it, Willie?
WILLIE: I've got more important things to worry about.
BEA: You mean the prowlers? Yes, I suppose you're right. The poem should be about the prowlers. End with the prowlers. They snarl in the bushes all right. Trample the ivy. Did you see the broken gutters? I'm certainly glad you're here, Willie. A woman needs her son in times like these.
WILLIE: [*Looking up at her.*] I do my job. Manly things. I do what's needed.
BEA: I'm glad someone does. I've even enlisted your sister in the cause. Dolores is hardly front-line material. Desperation makes the damnedest bedfellows. Where do you suppose she is now? Down in the basement watching TV, that's where. Her day off. I think she's part mole. Hardly comes up anymore. Lives and breathes in the dark.

[*She knocks on* WILLIE's *head.*] Are you alive in there? Are you listening?

[WILLIE *continues to oil the gun.* BEA *walks to the stove. She picks up a teacup.*]

    Is this stuff supposed to be so green? Do you know anything about tea? It looks like it's fermenting. Growing in the cup. Mold. Penicillin. It'll kill almost anything.
WILLIE: I'm going to kill them.
BEA: [*Studying* WILLIE.] I went wrong somewhere. Maybe the wrong kind of toilet training. Should have consulted an astrologer. Should have remarried. The first man I could get my hands on. Your father's mortician. Any man. Found me a weasel or a rat. Right, Willie? [*She snaps her fingers in front of his face.*] Talk to me, Willie. I'm confused. I need your help.
WILLIE: If you look at it in the right light, Mother, the present crisis can build nerves of steel. I'm taking ROTC in school. I can apply theoretical knowledge to a practical situation. That's why I'm here, Mother. I'm going to kill the prowlers. *Your* prowlers. But not yet. I ran from the car to the front door. Threw them off-guard. Toying with them. The rifle hidden between my legs. Never raise a gun unless you intend to use it. I learned that in school.
BEA: They've been scaring the hell out of me. Tapping on the windows. Rooting in the garden. Hanging outside my bedroom window. How many are out there now?
WILLIE: I was running. It's hard to run and count at the same time.
BEA: I don't trust myself anymore, Willie. No perspective. I'm too involved with my own life.
WILLIE: What life? Involved in what?
BEA: My art. You weren't listening. My work has come alive. It scares me. Like the prowlers. Everything is seething with life around here.
WILLIE: Remember the practical things, Mother. I'm the Captain of my rifle squad. That's why I'm here.
BEA: I write poems. In spite of adversity, I write. Adversity inspires me.
WILLIE: I tried to write poems. Once. Love poems to my rifle. Squadrons of poems.
BEA: [*Pointing to gun.*] Do you have to be so damn Freudian with that thing? Something starts creeping inside me. [*She looks at him suspiciously.*] Motherly love? No, not anymore. The last line, damnit. The definitive ode to the prowlers.

[WILLIE *aims his gun at the sink. Whenever he fires the gun, he makes the rifle's noise himself.*]

WILLIE: Pow. Pow. Blew his head off.

BEA: Don't shoot the china. It's hard to replace. Dolores broke two cups last week. Jumped out of her hands.
WILLIE: Don't let that cretin touch anything. Too bad being a brother means you're related. Maybe we can hang her from the upstairs window as bait. [*He aims gun through the imaginary window over the audience.*] Don't worry. The gun's not loaded. That was the second thing they told us: Never carry a loaded gun. Pay attention to the prowlers, Mother. The present danger. Stop writing those poems. You have responsibilities, too.
BEA: I need help, Willie. Not cops and robbers. I'm confused. You're as bad as Dolores with her doll. A thirty-year-old woman still playing grown-up. What's she waiting for?
WILLIE: A woman can't ever be too safe. [*PAUSE*] Last week in class we got to shoot cardboard figures. We aim right below the heart. [*He aims the gun below* BEA's *heart.*] There's some vital organ in there that's almost impossible to kill. It's the key to life. That's where you're suppose to aim. It's where all the feeling comes from. Floods the body with emotions. You have to be a crack shot to kill that gland. [*He "shoots"* BEA.] Pow. Pow. You're dead. [BEA *deflects the gun with her hand.*] Next week they're going to show us that gland. An organ that died too early—floating in a bottle. Not for the squeamish, that's for sure. One of our required courses is body parts. They're going to show us where to shoot.
BEA: I don't remember you being interested in firearms before.
WILLIE: Always. Even when I was much smaller. A tiny man. Nothing to do. I'd hang out waiting for the waterbugs. In the dark. They would crawl over my feet. Pretending to be friendly. But their little legs would get caught in my socks. At first I would pull their legs off. Smash them with my Keds.
BEA: I couldn't watch you all the time. I had to have a few minutes to myself.
WILLIE: But when I was old enough I bought a gun. A BB gun. I hid it from you. I can hide things well. Now I don't have to. [WILLIE *scans the floor with the gun.*] I stand there patiently in the dark. I like to surprise them. I'm afraid, but that makes it more exciting. Not knowing when they'll come. How many there'll be. Then suddenly I sense them. [WILLIE *stands.*] They assemble around my feet like I was a great stone god. Natives who have come to worship. They bring me their offerings. Bread crumbs. Lint. Then I flick on the light. The look of terror on their ugly, trusting little faces! I am no longer their great, safe stone god in the dark. I am a human monster. Glorious. Dangerous. What I was meant to be. I revel in my humanity. They run. They can be fast. You would be too, if moved by the fear of God or death. But I'm faster. Sleek. Lethal. I can let

them have it right between the eyes. There isn't much left when I get done with them. Pathetic little bodies splattered all over the floor. I know exactly who I am—the great white hunter. [PAUSE] Now I'm ready for bigger game. [WILLIE sits.]

BEA: God, you make me nervous.

WILLIE: Violence is a form of therapy. Don't let anyone tell you differently. [Loud knocking off-stage. PAUSE.] Prowlers?

BEA: They're everywhere. Dolores can't take care of them anymore. She's nervous. Like one of those dogs nodding in the back of old Chevrolets. Your sister always did have us beat in the screw-loose department.

[WILLIE moves his gun rapidly along the floor, as if chasing waterbugs.]

WILLIE: Pow. Pow. I'm here, Mother. There's a man in the house again. Twenty years of living on this planet is twenty years of preparation. The first prowler that appears . . .

BEA: I wrote you to help me get a perspective on things. Put things in their proper compartments. I didn't expect a hired killer.

WILLIE: [Looking out of imaginary window.] There. Running across the backyard. About 5-10. Non-descript face. He's gone. They're fast. Moved by fear of the Almighty. Desperate creatures. There he goes again. [WILLIE shoots through the window.] Pow. Pow. Missed. Shit. [Loud knocking off-stage.] Are they trying to get into the basement?

[WILLIE aims at BEA's head.]

BEA: For God's sake, Willie, put that damn thing down. Talk to me.

WILLIE: [Aiming gun over audience.] Should I blow their heads off one-by-one or stand back and go for the scatter effect?

BEA: I didn't raise you to be a ghoul. [PAUSE] I need time to think. I need inspiration to finish my poem. Too many distractions. The muse is here and gone before I've had a chance to shake her hand. Willie, I need a last line for that poem! [PAUSE] Maybe we should talk to them. Reason with them. Ask questions.

WILLIE: Shoot first ask questions later.

BEA: Think Willie. Everybody has their reasons. Everyone's possessed in their own way. You should console an artist in her old . . . *middle* years.

WILLIE: Aren't I doing that now? [WILLIE shoots.] Pow. Look. They're appearing like in one of those shooting galleries. Little crosses that pop up when you least expect it. Moving targets. Pow. Pow. You're dead. Then I win the big stuffed bear.

BEA: It's all right, Willie. Let me hold your hand. Your trigger-happy fingers. Maybe we need professional help. I can call some kind of exterminator. They're prompt. And efficient.

WILLIE: We don't need outsiders. Competition! I'm trained to kill.
BEA: Maybe I could read them one of my love poems. That would calm them. "Ode to Desperate Living." A woman is not completely lost as long as she has her art. [*The knocks become louder.*]
WILLIE: What's Dolores doing? Can't she hear that racket?
BEA: She's confused. Distracted. She forgets where she is. She and her doll. She doesn't do what she's told. There should be an understanding between a mother and a daughter. Something sacred. [WILLIE *puts the gun into his mouth.*] You're pretty attached to that thing, aren't you? [BEA *pulls it out of his mouth.*] You read too much as a kid. Cowboys and Indians. Rescue the damsel in distress. I can see now that the rescue I need isn't in your arsenal. [WILLIE *sticks the gun in his ear.*] Son, you're already a hero in your mother's eyes. You may not be all together upstairs, but I'm still proud of you. Is that what you want to hear? [BEA *takes gun from* WILLIE.] Maybe I can solve this thing by myself. You might even go back to school. [WILLIE *grabs the gun back.*] That is, if you want. Maybe you should talk to your sister. She's an example. Knows how to take things in her stride. [*She calls.*] Dolores!
WILLIE: Remember when I was a kid? A teensy-weensy man.
BEA: [*Calling.*] Dolores! Your brother's home.
WILLIE: Remember how you thought I was afraid of the dark. I had a Bozo nightlight. You made me wear pajamas with Day-Glo bunnies on them.
BEA: You're like your father, Willie. [WILLIE *smiles.*] Innocuous, but well-meaning. He never intended to hurt anyone. Never intended to die. He intended to live forever.

[DOLORES, *30, appears in the basement door wearing an old raincoat, curlers in her hair, mismatched socks, garish make-up and balances the remains of a sloppy breakfast tray on one arm. When she speaks, she does so in a rapid manner. Neither* BEA *nor* WILLIE *are aware that she's there.*]

BEA: Life warps you like a piece of plywood paneling. It's subtle. You go through life trying to walk the straight and narrow, but all the time you're on a slant. [*Calling nervously.*] Dolores!

[WILLIE *raises the gun over the audience.*]

WILLIE: There's another one. Pow. Pow. They're everywhere. Blots on the landscape. Completely surrounding the house. We'll have to shoot our way out.
BEA: Son, why don't you go back to school. I can take care of myself. [*Calling angrily.*] Dolores!
DOLORES: [*Startling* BEA.] There's so much noise around here. No way to think. The prowlers were knocking on the window. I told them I

was watching *The Guiding Light.* "No" was definitely not in their vocabulary. That knocking can get on your nerves. You miss the plot. What do you want, Mother?

BEA: Call me Bea. It's better for morale. Say "hello" to your brother. It appears he's come home [*Nervous, business-like.*] I think we need some outside perspective. That's why I called you up here, Dolores. Your brother's a "delicate" boy. We're in the middle of a "delicate" conversation.

DOLORES: You see, Mom . . . Bea. Some people have a philosophy of life. I've got a cooking philosophy. I divide the whole world into those who use meat extenders and those who don't. I mean, if you can't help out a little hamburger . . .

BEA: . . . then who can you help. I know. I've heard it before. I've raised the Nietzsche of the kitchen.

[WILLIE *moves away from the window. He points the gun at* DOLORES.]

WILLIE: Dolores, we've got real problems now. Nobody can get out of the house.

BEA: [*Whispering to* WILLIE.] Cut that out, Willie. Desperation's the one thing we have to guard against. You have a frontier mentality. Doesn't this look like a civilized kitchen to you? Trash masher. Cuisinart. You can't scare Dolores. She's your sister.

WILLIE: [*Whispering.*] I can threaten her if I want to. Even if she is my sister. *Especially* if she's my sister. That's what she's here for. To be bossed around. To be threatened. To be beaten within an inch of her life. She isn't on the front lines. I'm in charge now. I know what the problem is. I know what to do. We have enough problems without worrying about morale.

BEA: [*Whispering.*] Willie, try to say something nice for a change. I don't want her to panic.

WILLIE: [*Whispering.*] She doesn't look scared to me.

BEA: [*Whispering.*] She hides it. Talk to her, Willie.

WILLIE: [*Whispering.*] Why? She's hired help now. A foot soldier. I don't even know what common people talk about.

BEA: [*Whispering.*] Sex and celebrities, for God's sake. Just like everybody else. Talk to her!

DOLORES: [*Whispering, playing with food.*] Are you two done? [*PAUSE, then chattily.*] Well, I was lying there minding my own business. Then they started knocking again. It's annoying when you're trying to get two thoughts together. What was I thinking about? Oh yes. One of the orderlies back at the hospital. I had crushes on all of them. I was just staring at the remains of my nice Tuesday morning *day off* breakfast tray. Thinking of Clinton, the orderly. My orderly. I always make a breakfast tray for myself *on my day off,* Bea. What was on the plate? I can tell you that right off. It's sitting right in front of me. Two eggs fried hard. Baked beans. Beef liver. Toast. Half of a tuna pot pie. Well, I was just lying there smoking one of my Lucky Strikes when what do you think happened?

BEA: I don't know. Neither of us knows. Get on with it, Dolores.

DOLORES: Well, all of a sudden a spider swooped down out of the cobwebs and carried off a piece of buttered whole wheat toast. Imagine that.

WILLIE: Did you see any prowlers?

DOLORES: No two-legged ones. But there's hundreds of waterbugs down there. It's like the outside, except that it's inside. Pretty soon there'll be moss growing over my vanity table. Snakes in my drawers. Those little buggies squirm all over my face at night. Crawl through my dreams, turning them into nightmares. I don't like to think about it. I don't like to think about anything at all. It's easier that way.

BEA: That's very interesting, young lady. But the fact of the matter is that we're trying to have a very important conversation. The old give and take. Willie and I were talking about safety. How to live through the night. If you have any thoughts on the matter . . . No. Go and fix yourself another piece of toast. Take your time.

[DOLORES *begins to rock back and forth in her chair. A fit.*]

WILLIE: Anything for attention. [*PAUSE. He watches her closely.*] That girl gives me the creeps. I don't care if we are related. She's like an evil thought. Suicide. Playing with yourself. Sometimes bad thoughts just hang around in my brain. No place to go. Murder. She terrifies me.

BEA: Sometimes she terrifies me, Willie. I gave a formal dinner party. Dolores was serving the Halibut Cheese Surprise, McCall's Dinner Recipe Find No. 38. Are you listening? There's a point to this story. She went into one of her little rocking fits. I was mortified. She held the serving platter in her hands and was standing over the guest of honor, a female private detective. Did you know that female private eyes are called dickless Tracys? Well, I invited her over to case out the prowlers. Imagine! Dolores was standing over Tracy rocking the entree. Tracy kept trying to grab a piece of halibut as it rocked by. I tried to hold Dolores long enough to flip a piece off onto Tracy's plate. Finally, Dolores knocked the fish off the platter and fell down on the carpet. Halibut juice all over her face.

WILLIE: Why don't you get rid of her?

BEA: That is not the point of the story, Willie. The point is that Dolores is your sister. I'm responsible for her. We both are. She's like your father's side of the family. Obscure relatives. Inbreeding. We're all related by incest. And it's up to all of us to do something. Anything.

This is a *family* crisis. We need a *family* solution. But at this point, I'll take anything I can get. If you're going back to school, Willie . . . [*Knocking begins again.*] Excuse me. I'd better check that.

[BEA *leaves the room.* WILLIE *hangs a BB target around* DOLORES' *neck, with some difficulty because she's still rocking. Slowly, he takes aim.*]

WILLIE: Here's my cure for mental illness.

[*The knocking stops.* BEA *returns and sees what's happening. She shrieks, flings herself across* DOLORES' *chest, both rocking together.*]

BEA: What do you think you're doing? Where does it say that you can take fate into your own hands? Fate has a mind of its own. Shoot at the prowlers if you have to, but Dolores is your sister. You can choose your friends, Willie, but you've got your relatives for life. You might as well get used to that. [BEA *slaps* DOLORES *across the face.*] If Mother Nature doesn't bring her around, this mother usually can. [DOLORES *stops rocking.*] If I startled you, Dolores, I'm sorry. I'm glad you were sitting down. Take a breather. [*They all relax. A tremendous knock off-stage.* BEA *jumps.*] Shit.

[WILLIE *grabs his gun.*]

WILLIE: They're coming into the basement. I'm going down.

[BEA *pushes* WILLIE *away and grabs his gun.*]

BEA: I'll take care of this. I always have and I always will. [*PAUSE*] They're my prowlers.

[BEA *runs out of the room. There is a strained silence between* WILLIE *and* DOLORES.]

DOLORES: [*Groggily.*] Where am I?
WILLIE: In the kitchen. In trouble. [*PAUSE*] You never liked me very much, did you Dolores? Even when we were little, we never talked. You picked on me. You used to beat me up once a week. Remember?
DOLORES: I've got better things to do than wonder if you're worth talking to. Where's Mother?
WILLIE: [*Standing close to* DOLORES.] In the basement. Protecting us, she thinks. She said to ask you about sex or celebrities while she was gone. Do you have any thoughts on either?
DOLORES: [*Playing up to* WILLIE.] Well, my favorite celebrity is Loretta Lynn. A real hard-luck case. But I suppose sex makes for better conversation. That's what I think about when I have my fits. Sex. Sex of my own free will. I came out of electro-shock a little confused about the facts of life. That's when I met Clinton. Best sex of my life. Crazy. Wild. Romantic. Hung like a horse. He pulled out just in

(From the Yale Drama School production)

WILLIE: Here's my cure for mental illness.

time, too. Lately, though, I've had trouble remembering. Those damn prowlers have screwed up everything.

[*The rifle goes off in the basement—the sound of a real shot.* WILLIE *gasps. SILENCE.* BEA *enters, holding a large male doll with a big bullethole in its middle.*]

BEA: My God, Willie. I thought this thing wasn't loaded. I scared myself to death. I could've hurt someone.

[WILLIE *grabs his gun back.*]

WILLIE: Just one bullet. Just in case. When things get out of hand. Out of control. Russsian roulette. I was waiting for the right day to try it out. A nice bright spring day. Robins puking their guts out. April, maybe. Looks like I won't get my chance.

DOLORES: [*Moaning.*] Clinton! [*Holding up her doll.*] Something is definitely wrong with my little Clinton.

WILLIE: What happened down there?

BEA: I couldn't help it. Suddenly I wasn't myself. I was someone else for a split second, looking back at myself. I was someone I didn't know existed. Big blank eyes. I saw them reflected in the window. I reacted without thinking. I shot Dolores' doll.

DOLORES: [*Cradling doll.*] Murderer. You murderer.

[BEA *starts to take the doll away.*]

Don't take him away from me, Mother. Bea. I can still love him as he is. Even with that hole in his middle. Clinton gave him to me as a good luck present when I left the hospital. It's all I have to remember him by. An orderly loved me. So I loved his doll back. I named him Clinton. Naming means love, Bea. Now Clinton's dead. I have to start looking for another Clinton. Start looking for someone to love.

BEA: For God's sake, Dolores, give me that . . .that . . . thing.

[BEA *grabs the doll.*]

DOLORES: [*Angrily.*] You always ruin everything, Mother. You'll never be yourself until you're dead. If you ask me, people should start dead.

BEA: [*Angrily.*] As bad as it is, Dolores, just stick to the cooking. Great steaming masses of unidentifiable vegetables. That's your forte. Leave the poetry to me! Leave everything to me! I've always taken care of you, Dolores. But now it's time to take care of myself. [*PAUSE*] When all this is over, I'm going to Switzerland. I read about this new thing over there. It's called sleep therapy. What you do is lay down in a comfortable hospital bed and they do the rest. You sleep and sleep and sleep. The world passes you by, but who

cares? You can finally get some rest. When you wake up, say in a year or two, you're a different person. You're the person you were meant to be. I want to be the person I was meant to be.
DOLORES: I can look for someone for you to love too, Mother.

[*PAUSE.* BEA *pours Scotch in three tea cups.*]

BEA: A toast. To the prowlers. There's no stopping them now.
WILLIE: You think that's the answer.
DOLORES: Mother deserves a chance too, Willie. I could fix one of them dinner. You wouldn't have to do anything. A prowler could eat right at this table. In the father's chair. Like Goldilocks and the Three Bears. A prowler wouldn't eat much. Wouldn't say much. It would be a nice dinner.
WILLIE: [*To* BEA.] You'd let one of the prowlers into this house?
BEA: Am I going to have a choice? Besides, there's something . . . reassuring about new faces.
DOLORES: Maybe we could start a family again.
BEA: No. Definitely not a family. Maybe just throwing open the doors and welcoming them is the answer.

[BEA *opens the basement door.*]

WILLIE: [*Raising gun.*] I'll welcome them.
DOLORES: With sleeping bags and cots we could find places for them to stay. I'm sure they wouldn't mind the basement. At least it's inside. Warm near the furnace. They wouldn't be much trouble, Willie.
WILLIE: They wouldn't be much trouble dead.
BEA: Men have always done what they wanted. Shoot first, isn't that right, Willie? But as for us, young lady, we've got work to do.
DOLORES: [*Walking to the window.*] I'm going back to the basement. I'll hose it down and set up the cots. Make it nice. Throw pillows. Individual name tags. Since they're coming, they should be comfortable. [*Waving out of window.*] Welcome to a clean basement!

[DOLORES *exits with her doll.* WILLIE *slams the door behind her. He points his gun at* BEA.]

WILLIE: How can I ever trust you again, Mother? Aren't you for law and order? You call me home to rescue you, but you're ready to invite the enemy in. You really like facing death at every turn. It makes you feel alive. What about me? How can I feel alive? [*PAUSE. Vehemently.*] No prowler's going to love me. [*Motioning at* BEA *with gun.*] Pow. Pow. You're dead. [*PAUSE*]
BEA: I've never felt so useful.
WILLIE: Mother, can't you see we're in danger here. We're all in mortal danger.

BEA: Willie, listen to me. I'm not going to fight the prowlers anymore. I've got to put myself back together. Like a jigsaw puzzle. I've got to find two pieces that fit. [*PAUSE*] What if a prowler ate dinner here? What harm would it do? What if we went further? . . .
WILLIE: [*Interrupting.*] Tell me I didn't just hear that. There, I clicked my ears off. I don't hear a thing. [*PAUSE. Suddenly.*] Would he sleep in your bed? On the family sheets? Press his head against the rose-patterned pillow slips? My God, do you realize you'd be consorting with the enemy?

[*At one of the imaginary windows,* WILLIE *raises his gun over the audience.* BEA *stands behind him.* WILLIE *shoots.*]

WILLIE: Pow. [*PAUSE*]
BEA: [*Quietly.*] Your small fur-covered body/pressed smooth against my side.

[*PAUSE.* BEA *walks to the other imaginary window. As the stage lights slowly dim,* BEA *and* WILLIE *appear in their own spotlights at their own windows.*]

BEA: I made a mistake trying to finish that poem. Searching for a last line from all the possible last lines in the world. The poem had an ending all along: my prowlers. Standing at my window, his face pressed against the glass.
WILLIE: [*Shooting.*] Pow. Got another one. The practical things, Mother. It's almost over. I'll get all of them and then I'll leave. [*Shooting.*] Pow. Pow.
BEA: He doesn't want to hurt me. He's just waiting. Waiting for me to open the window.
WILLIE: [*Shooting.*] Pow. Got another one, Mother. Pow. Pow. Look at that. Blood over the grass, Mother. A fountain of blood. Blood dripping from the trees. The flowers. Pow. Pow. Pow. A bloodbath.
BEA: Tonight when he comes I'll open the window and I'll be rescued. That familiar face will never go away. All the features are clear. Complete. A perfect fit, my face over his.
WILLIE: It's all right, Mother. I'm here. There's only one more.

[*His gun follows something outside the window.*]

BEA: [*Tentatively waving out the window.*] The perfect guest. Perfect together, no longer alone. Rescued. I'll prepare him a feast. I'll serve him from my best china. I'll sleep with him, too. You might even say we'll make love. A gift to myself. Entwined in each other's arms for the rest of my life.
WILLIE: But I'm here. I'm here, Mother.
BEA: Rescued? [*PAUSE*] Yes. I'm glad you're home, Willie.

[WILLIE *shoots.*]

WILLIE: Pow.

[*He misses.*]

    Shit. [*PAUSE*] I'm aiming. I'm giving it my best shot, Mother. He's running toward the house. Perfect. The last perfect shot.

[WILLIE *moves the gun rapidly, as if following the prowler. He shoots again.*]

    Pow.

[BEA *falls to the floor. PAUSE.*]

    Got him.

[*BLACKOUT*]

STRAWBERRY ENVY

(from the collection, TRIPLET)

by

KITTY JOHNSON

(The play was first presented at the Los Angeles Actors' Theatre's Festival of Premieres in 1983.)

Original Cast
(In Order of Appearance)

CRAIG	Scanlon Gail
EMILY	Laurie O'Brien
MAN IN WHITE	Granville van Deusen

Directed by .... Al Rossi
Produced by .... Adam Leipzig & Diane White

Bill Bushnell, Artistic Producing Director

Strawberry Envy

[*A roadside fruit and vegetable stand, more whimsical or stylistic than realistic. Perhaps painted indications of the various fruits, with signs indicating prices, etc. The strawberry section, however, is very special, and should be real.*

At rise, CRAIG, *the proprietor of the stand, is working on the strawberry display. A sign reads: "Strawberries: Special—Today Only $1.59/quart."*

Unnoticed by him, an incredibly handsome MAN IN WHITE *enters on his shiny white bicycle.* EMILY *is on the handlebars. They pedal past the stand and exit while disagreeing about the strawberries.*]

EMILY: Oh, look! Craig's runnin' a special. . . .
MAN IN WHITE: Not today, darling. We really don't have the time.

[*The* MAN IN WHITE *is immaculately dressed—white suit, buckskin shoes, etc. and perhaps a red tie and red socks.* EMILY *is attractive, but not spectacular, has light red hair and pale skin. She's probably in her midthirties.*

As CRAIG *continues fussing with his display,* EMILY *and* MAN IN WHITE *bicycle back onto stage—she has won the argument, bits of which were heard offstage before their reappearance—"But you know how I love strawberries," "You're so impetuous," etc. Finally they come to a halt in front of the stand.*]

EMILY: Stop here!
MAN IN WHITE: You know, of course, that I am only stopping because your slightest wish is my command—as they say.
EMILY: Of course.
MAN IN WHITE: But Emily, my pet, there will be plenty of strawberries in Lexington. I don't see why we have to stop here. What if we miss the bus?
EMILY: I'll only be the smallest of moments. I promise.
MAN IN WHITE: You are incredibly lovely.
EMILY: Thank you. So are you.
MAN IN WHITE: I know.
EMILY: [*To* CRAIG] Hi, Craig!

[CRAIG *who has been oblivious to all that has transpired, looks up to* EMILY *for the first time. He does not notice the* MAN IN WHITE.]

CRAIG: Emily!
EMILY: I just happened to be passing by. . . on my way to Lexington . . . and noticed you're runnin' a special. How thoroughly delightful.

CRAIG: The usual quart?
EMILY: Oh, dear. I'm not that predictable?
MAN IN WHITE: Would you mind terribly if I kissed you?
CRAIG: I think predictable is the last word anyone would use to describe you, ma'am.
EMILY: Thank you. You certainly know how to make a woman feel like a woman.
CRAIG: Yeah. That's what mom always said.
MAN IN WHITE: I've offended you, haven't I? Please forgive me.
EMILY: [*To* MAN IN WHITE—CRAIG *does not hear*] No. No. You haven't offended me at all.
CRAIG: You all right, ma'am?
EMILY: Of course.
CRAIG: You keep lookin' around like you might be expectin' someone.
EMILY: Oh, no. It's just us. Me and You.
CRAIG: Oh.
EMILY: That doesn't frighten you, does it?
CRAIG: Oh, no.
EMILY: Good.
CRAIG: Should it?
EMILY: Of course not. And to show you just how madcap and unpredictable I really am, I shall change my order. Yes. Today I want two quarts of strawberries.
MAN IN WHITE: I know I've offended you.
CRAIG: Sure you can handle it?
EMILY: Aren't you even the teeniest bit curious as to why I want so many strawberries today?
CRAIG: Okay. I'll bite. Why do you want so many?
EMILY: To keep me company on the bus. I hate travelling alone.
MAN IN WHITE: But, what about me?
CRAIG: Ah, the bus to Lexington.
EMILY: Exactly.
MAN IN WHITE: I've blown it, haven't I? I was just so overcome with desire. I should have waited for a more propitious moment. A woman of your obvious discretion requires something more subtle. Got to think of something subtle.
EMILY: [*To* CRAIG] I'd prefer to go to California, of course, but I can't take the sun there. It goes right to my head. And it's a very long bus ride. [*She looks at bike*] I wish I had a bicycle. You don't by any chance have a bicycle, do you?
MAN IN WHITE: Subtle . . . subtle. . . .
CRAIG: No, but I've got the pick-up in the back if you need a lift somewhere.

EMILY: Oh, no. No, no. That's all right. I was just thinkin' how nice it might be to ride a bicycle all the way to Lexington. The bus gets so stifling sometimes.
MAN IN WHITE: I love you madly!
CRAIG: Sounds like fun.
EMILY: Oh! Then you must come with me. Some Saturday perhaps. Just for the day. Throw caution to the wind and let the stand run itself.
CRAIG: You'd better stop goin' on like that, ma'am. I just might take you up on one of your crazy offers someday.
EMILY: The grass there is truly blue.
MAN IN WHITE: Like your eyes.
EMILY: Like in the postal cards. They say it's supposed to be blue in the entire state, of course, but it's been my experience that it's bluest in Lexington. I try to get down there at least once or twice a year.
CRAIG: Well, I want you to know I think it's great the way you travel around like that. Do things on your own. I don't think you're weird at all.
EMILY: Weird?
MAN IN WHITE: He's the one who's weird, Emily.
CRAIG: Not weird, exactly. What's the word they use these days? Spaced!
MAN IN WHITE: Spaced!
CRAIG: That's it! Spaced! I don't think you're spaced at all.
EMILY: I'm not quite sure I'm followin' you here. Weird? Spaced?
CRAIG: You know how people talk. . . .
EMILY: I'm sure I don't.
CRAIG: Sorry. I'll just get your strawberries.
MAN IN WHITE: Yes. Let me feed you a strawberry!
EMILY: [*To both*] Thank you.

[MAN IN WHITE *picks out a nice strawberry and gives it to* EMILY. *She studies it with great longing.*]

CRAIG: It's the height of the season.
MAN IN WHITE: It certainly is.
EMILY: Have you ever heard of a place called the Imperial Valley? Doesn't that sound just too exotic? It's in California. I hear tell the strawberries there grow to two, three times the size of these.
MAN IN WHITE: Mmmm.
CRAIG: But do they have the flavor of my Kentucky strawberries?
EMILY: Oh, not for one minute was I trying to slander your strawberries, Craig. They are lovely. Truly they are.
MAN IN WHITE: But not nearly as lovely as you.
EMILY: I like to run my tongue over 'em, real slow like. [*She does so.*] They're smooth and rough at the same time.

CRAIG: I really wish you wouldn't do that in front of me, ma'am.
EMILY: I wonder if you have any idea how truly wonderful your strawberries are? Have you ever tried one? I mean really tried one? I bet you just pop 'em in your mouth without even tastin' 'em.
CRAIG: Truth to tell, I never cared for 'em that much.

[As EMILY *begins to run her tongue over the strawberry again,* MAN IN WHITE *suddenly takes her into his arms, dips her and kisses her passionately.* EMILY *tries desperately to maintain her equilibrium.*]

EMILY: [*To* CRAIG] The . . . uh . . . height of the season, you say?
CRAIG: Absolutely.
EMILY: A full quart, then.
CRAIG: Just the one?
EMILY: I feel like splurgin'. And don't sneak any of the rotten ones into the bottom.
CRAIG: I'd never do a thing like that to you, ma'am.
EMILY: I hate rotten strawberries.

[CRAIG'S *back is turned as he packs the strawberries for* EMILY.]

MAN IN WHITE: Oh Emily. You are far too sensitive for these minor hassles of daily existence. You deserve better. Let me take you away with me. To New Zealand. We can grow our very own strawberries.
EMILY: Do they grow strawberries in New Zealand?
CRAIG: Some of the best.
EMILY: [*To* MAN IN WHITE] Why don't you loosen your tie?
MAN IN WHITE: Anything you say, my sweet.
CRAIG: You thinkin' of goin' there?
EMILY: [*To* CRAIG] Now what would people say if I suddenly upped and ran off to New Zealand with you? That would hardly be proper. Although it is quite temptin'.
CRAIG: I told you not to talk like that!
EMILY: Yes. Of course. I must have been thinkin' of . . .
MAN IN WHITE: Shall we go to my villa? Sit by the fire, sip . . .
EMILY: . . . strawberry daiquiris . . .
MAN IN WHITE: It's yours. I shall prepare them myself. With fresh strawberries. And we'll read poetry. Your poetry, perhaps.
EMILY: Yes! I'll sell the chili parlor and become a great poet!
MAN IN WHITE: You've got the right name for it. Emily. Like Emily Dickenson. American. Eighteen-thirty, eighteen-eighty-six.
CRAIG: Sometimes I really wonder about you.
EMILY: But I can't make a livin' writin' poetry.
MAN IN WHITE: Who needs money when you have love?
EMILY: True.
MAN IN WHITE: Oh, Emily, dear Emily . . . / Shall I compare thee to

a Strawberry?/ With lips of red and tender touch/ Sweet juices that I love so much.
CRAIG: Well, anyway, that'll be a buck fifty-nine.
EMILY: Money, yes, of course. Let me just . . .
CRAIG: Ma'am? Are you all right? You aren't havin' one of your spells, are you?
EMILY: Spells?
CRAIG: Well, you know . . .
EMILY: That's what you mean by weird? I have spells?
CRAIG: I didn't mean it as an insult. I was just worried.
EMILY: I suppose you have never had a daydream? That's what I have, you know. Daydreams.
MAN IN WHITE: My love.
EMILY: Very vivid daydreams.
MAN IN WHITE: My precious.
EMILY: Everybody has daydreams.
MAN IN WHITE: My angel.
EMILY: Don't they?
CRAIG: Not me.
EMILY: You're kidding. In all your life you've never had a dream?
MAN IN WHITE: You, my sweet, are the answer to all dreams.
CRAIG: Of course I've had dreams. Everybody dreams.
EMILY: Aha!
CRAIG: But at night. When I'm asleep. Not in the middle of the day.
EMILY: But surely there must be things you, shall we say, want . . .
MAN IN WHITE: Desire.
EMILY: . . . very much, but you'll probably never have, but still you like to think about what it must be like. . . .
CRAIG: Not that I recall.
EMILY: And just when I was beginnin' to kind of like you.
MAN IN WHITE: Him?
EMILY: [*To* MAN IN WHITE] And why not?
MAN IN WHITE: Oh, nothing. Perhaps I overestimated your taste level.
CRAIG: Although, now that you mention it, I do sometimes wonder what it must be like to be, I don't know . . . something else besides a truck farmer. Not that I don't love my work. I do. But I don't get to meet many people, like you must over at the chili parlor.
EMILY: [*To* MAN IN WHITE] I wonder if you could just go stand over there next to him for a moment?
MAN IN WHITE: With pleasure. I think you'll see what I mean.
EMILY: There is a slight resemblance.
MAN IN WHITE: This is too amusing. It's the sun, Emily. The sun. You can't take the sun. It's altering your perception.
EMILY: [*To* CRAIG] Have you ever considered wearing your hair with a part?

[EMILY *fixes* CRAIG'S *hair to look like* MAN IN WHITE'S, *using the latter as a model.*]

CRAIG: What are you doing?
EMILY: Not bad.
MAN IN WHITE: Ridiculous.
EMILY: Not bad at all.
CRAIG: I don't like my hair like that.
EMILY: But it's very becoming.
MAN IN WHITE: Not really.
CRAIG: Hey, stop. Okay?
MAN IN WHITE: This guy has no class, Emily. Whatsoever.
EMILY: [*To* CRAIG] What did I do?
CRAIG: You start ramblin' on about your daydreams . . . which, by the way, even if I do think about things bein' different, I don't get spells and say I see 'em or anything like you do, and then . . . then you start messin' around with my hair. I changed my mind. You are weird.
EMILY: Well, then. You can just keep your stupid strawberries, if that's the way you're gonna be. Who wants 'em, anyway? Probably not even organic.
MAN IN WHITE: Let's get out of here. We've got a bus to catch.
EMILY: Yes. I have a bus to catch.

[EMILY *and* MAN IN WHITE *head for the bicycle.*]

CRAIG: I didn't mean to make you mad. I just get nervous when people touch me like that. I'm not used to it.
EMILY: You're probably allergic to strawberries, too.
CRAIG: I just don't happen to like 'em.

[CRAIG *throws the berries back into the bin, somewhat violently.*]

EMILY: You'll bruise them!!

[MAN IN WHITE *suddenly gasps as if enthralled.* EMILY *mimics his gasp and follows his gaze, not knowing what it is about, but nonetheless carried away.*]

MAN IN WHITE: If you could see the way the sun falls on your hair! [*This does the trick*—EMILY'S *attention returns to him.*] Look! Every strand is a different color. Copper. Gold. Bronze. Strawberry. Grey.
EMILY: My hair is not grey!
CRAIG: Ma'am?
EMILY: Uh . . . in this light, do you think?
CRAIG: That's what I mean. You talk about one thing and then you start switchin' subjects. It's real hard keepin' up with you.
MAN IN WHITE: Sorry. Silver. Not grey. Silver. Platinum.

EMILY: You must be very careful with strawberries, you know. They're delicate. [*She fondles a strawberry*]
MAN IN WHITE: Like you. [*He fondles her*]
CRAIG: Strawberries are part of my business. Of course I'm careful.
EMILY: Offhand, Craig, what would you say is the most . . . passionate fruit of all?
MAN IN WHITE: Peaches.
CRAIG: Peaches.
EMILY: Peaches! Yes! And strawberries! You see how bright and juicy they are? How they just sit there and tempt you to pieces?
CRAIG: I try to control myself.
EMILY: Nothing personal, Craig, but if you continually try to control yourself, you are going to get nowhere in this life. Absolutely nowhere.
MAN IN WHITE: Good point.
CRAIG: But I don't like strawberries. I told you that.
EMILY: That's where you and I differ. I love 'em. I wait around all year for the season to start and then eat 'em up just as fast as they can grow. And just when I kind of get used to havin' 'em around . . . poof! [MAN IN WHITE *takes strawberry from her.*] They're gone. But it's always somethin' to look forward to, isn't it? Somethin' to remember.
CRAIG: I must be goin' crazy. I think I'm beginnin' to understand you.
EMILY: I just wish the season wasn't so damn short.
MAN IN WHITE: How about some whipped cream to go with those delicious strawberries?

[MAN IN WHITE *produces whipped cream, squirts it onto a strawberry.*]

EMILY: [*To* CRAIG] Perhaps I could persuade you to try just one? With whipped cream?
CRAIG: It almost sounds temptin', but . . . I'll just stick with my blackberries and peaches.
EMILY: Blackberries and pea . . . yes! Was that you? It was! You had a strawberry shortcake over at the chili parlor . . . you threw up all over the placemat. . . .
MAN IN WHITE: In his usual debonair manner.
CRAIG: It was the chili spagetti five way. Too spicy for me.
EMILY: It was the strawberries! You liked 'em so much but you were allergic! And then you said you'd better stick to blackberries and peaches from now on! My God, that must've been what, six, seven years ago. You even called me Ma'am. I remember.
CRAIG: I was hopin' you might have forgotten. I was so embarassed.
MAN IN WHITE: Oh, really?
CRAIG: I was afraid you'd never speak to me again.
EMILY: And you say *I'm* weird.

CRAIG: But there's nothin' wrong with peaches and blackberries, Emily. Look . . . [*He takes a peach*] They're so round. They just fit right into your hand like that's what it was made for.
EMILY: Yes. It is nice.
MAN IN WHITE: [*Unbuttoning Emily's blouse*] Oh, yes.
CRAIG: And it's soft.
MAN IN WHITE: [*Caressing Emily's breasts*] Very soft.
CRAIG: And still . . . firm.
MAN IN WHITE: Very firm.
CRAIG: And I love how when you split it open, the pit just sort of nestles there.
EMILY: Oh, yes.
MAN IN WHITE: You have the most beautiful breasts I have ever seen.
CRAIG: [*Biting into peach*] And I really can't think of anything more delicious.
MAN IN WHITE: Neither can I.

[EMILY *pushes* MAN IN WHITE's *face to her breast.*]

CRAIG: Except . . . maybe . . .
EMILY: Yes?
CRAIG: Oh, nothing . . . the peaches. They're so juicy.
EMILY: Oh.
CRAIG: What I really love . . . you won't tell anybody, will you?
EMILY: [*Quickly*] Of course not. What is it? [*To* MAN IN WHITE] A little to the left, please. [*Back to* CRAIG] What is it you really love?
CRAIG: It's how messy they are. How the juice just gets all over your hands and your mouth and your face and . . .
EMILY: You have quite an imagination yourself.
CRAIG: You think so?
EMILY: Uh, Craig. I'm just wonderin'. You know how the bathrooms are in those busses.
MAN IN WHITE: Oh, yes. Let's lock ourselves in the bathroom and make love at fifty-five miles an hour. Over these back Kentucky roads. We can feel every bump.
CRAIG: Ma'am?
MAN IN WHITE: We'll be near the motor. It'll rev up, then start to gasp and sputter, purr. Then we'll pull onto the Interstate and it'll be nice and smooth.
CRAIG: Are you doin' it now?
EMILY: Doin' what?
CRAIG: Havin' a spell? I don't mean it nasty like. I'm really interested. And you just sort of look like you're . . .
EMILY: Oh?
CRAIG: Well, I got so carried away talkin' about the peaches and all

... I almost felt like we . . . I mean, well . . . you were sayin' somethin' about the bathrooms on the busses?
EMILY: The . . . oh, yes. You know how you can never trust the water out of the taps on those things. I just wonder if you could possibly wash up the strawberries for me, before I take 'em on the bus? I don't want to take any chances.
CRAIG: Oh. You still want them?
EMILY: Oh, yes. Unpredictable me.

[CRAIG *packs up some berries and exits with them. The minute his back is turned,* EMILY *responds wholeheartedly to* MAN IN WHITE, *who begins to unbutton his shirt as* EMILY *unbuttons her blouse.*]

EMILY: Talk dirty to me.
MAN IN WHITE: Not now.
EMILY: In Italian.
MAN IN WHITE: I don't speak Italian.
EMILY: What?
MAN IN WHITE: No. Wait. I'm sorry. A few words. I might know a few words. Uh, mi amore . . .
EMILY: Oh, yes. Yes. Si. Ti voglio.
MAN IN WHITE: Mi amore.
EMILY: You said that already. Say something else.
MAN IN WHITE: Bellisima.
EMILY: Something dirty.
MAN IN WHITE: Aboslutely not.
EMILY: But you do want to do wicked things to my body.
MAN IN WHITE: I'm not sure I would phrase it exactly that way.
EMILY: How exactly would you phrase it?
MAN IN WHITE: What has come over you, Emily? You never used to be this aggressive.
EMILY: I cannot live my life in constant foreplay. I'm discussing the real thing here. And I want you to discuss it, too. In detail. In Italian.
MAN IN WHITE: I already told you I don't know any Italian.
EMILY: You have to speak Italian! You're my fantasy! You have to do what I say!
MAN IN WHITE: This is one fantasy with principles.
EMILY: Principles? You adore me. You'd do anything in the world for me. Fuck your principles.
MAN IN WHITE: You're too refined for that kind of talk. It's degrading.
EMILY: No, it's not. I like it. Really. It turns me on.
MAN IN WHITE: Turns you on? Can't you say something more poetic? Like . . . It ignites the buried flames of passion in my soul.
EMILY: Okay, okay. It ignites the buried flames of passion in my soul. Now, tell me again how great my tits are.

MAN IN WHITE: [*Rebuttoning shirt*] Forget it. You've spoiled the mood.
EMILY: You're mighty sassy today.

[CRAIG *re-enters with strawberries.*]

MAN IN WHITE: Why don't you ask him to speak Italian to you?
EMILY: [*To* CRAIG] Thank you. [*To* MAN IN WHITE] You're jealous!
MAN IN WHITE: Oh, Emily. You are so naive.
CRAIG: You're welcome.
MAN IN WHITE: Even if you do have some sort of perverted attraction for this guy, he is so limited. He could not, for example, bring you to ecstacy during rush hour at the chili parlor. People would look. But with me . . .
EMILY: I've never had anyone be jealous before. Will you fight a duel for me? [*To* CRAIG] Can you fence?
CRAIG: Excuse me?
MAN IN WHITE: For the record, I am not jealous.
EMILY: Ha!
CRAIG: I took some karate lessons down at the Y last summer.
EMILY: Oh?

[CRAIG *demonstrates clumsily but playfully, and* EMILY *tries to imitate him.* MAN IN WHITE *is aghast.*]

MAN IN WHITE: I am terribly disappointed in you. Getting yourself worked up over someone who's allergic to strawberries.
EMILY: You know, Craig. I've known you all these years . . . sort of . . . and I have absolutely never noticed how attractive you are.
MAN IN WHITE: Oh, please.
EMILY: I wonder why that is.
CRAIG: Oh, go on.
EMILY: I'd love to.
CRAIG: Uh, ma'am?
EMILY: Emily.
CRAIG: Ma'am?
EMILY: That's my name, remember? That's what you can call me instead of ma'am.
CRAIG: Okay, then. Emily.
EMILY: Oh! It sounds so nice the way you say it! Real poetic!
CRAIG: Uh, Emily . . . your blouse is open.
EMILY: I wonder how that could have happened! You did say you like peaches?
CRAIG: Very much.

[MAN IN WHITE *has had about as much as he can take.* EMILY *and* CRAIG *both become a little embarassed and pull away from each other.*]

MAN IN WHITE: Letting yourself be taken in because he happens to like peaches and then coming to me to satisfy your animal lust.
EMILY and CRAIG: [Together] Excuse me.
MAN IN WHITE: How do you think that makes me feel?
EMILY: [To CRAIG] So. How much do I owe you?
CRAIG: Buck fifty-nine.

[EMILY *finds money to pay him.*]

MAN IN WHITE: I'll tell you how it makes me feel, Emily. It makes me feel cheap. Cheap. And I don't appreciate it.
EMILY: Good price. Very good. Well worth every penny.
CRAIG: The way you talk about the strawberries, Emily, it almost makes me wish I wasn't allergic.
MAN IN WHITE: A strawberry farmer! Emily, really. [*Beat, as he changes his attitude, his confidence returns.*] Of course. One of those realistic, unimaginative types. Not your style at all. Nor, might I add, are you his.
EMILY: But I am incredibly lovely.
MAN IN WHITE: To me, yes. But to the average mortal . . .
EMILY: Thank you.
MAN IN WHITE: It's just that I, with my remarkable insight, am the only one who knows how incredibly lovely you truly are. In fact, I think you must be the loveliest of all.
EMILY: Of all? You mean there are others?
MAN IN WHITE: But none that compare to you.
CRAIG: They do look . . . like you said . . . bright and juicy.
EMILY: [*To* MAN IN WHITE, *ignoring* CRAIG] How many others?
MAN IN WHITE: You are not the only woman in the state of Kentucky who has spells, my darling. I am in great demand.
CRAIG: But they give me this terrible rash.
EMILY: [*To* MAN IN WHITE] But you always said that . . .
MAN IN WHITE: Although you do seem to need me more than anyone else I've run across to date. Maybe that's why I like you so much.
EMILY: I do not need anyone who refuses to learn a few simple Italian phrases.

[*She takes a strawberry from* CRAIG *and defiantly pops it into her mouth, then chokes on it, gasping for breath.* MAN IN WHITE *is immediately repentent.*]

MAN IN WHITE: Oh, my God, Emily? I'm sorry. Someone! Help! She's choking to death!

[CRAIG *is frozen to the spot and can barely manage to speak*]

CRAIG: Emily?

MAN IN WHITE: The ambulance drivers are on strike, Emily! I shall have to save you myself! [*He rushes ineptly to her aid.*] In goes the good air. Out goes the bad air. In goes the good air . . .

[CRAIG *manages to move, goes to her and pounds her clumsily on the back. She recovers.*]

EMILY: You can stop beating me now.
CRAIG: Are you all right?
EMILY: Strawberry. Wrong pipe.
CRAIG: God, I had visions of you goin' to the emergency ward down at County General.
EMILY: You did?
MAN IN WHITE: No. He's making it up.
CRAIG: Well, just for a minute.
MAN IN WHITE: Lying!
EMILY: Were they on strike?
CRAIG: What?
EMILY: The ambulance drivers. They were on strike? And you had to personally save my life?
MAN IN WHITE: *I* personally saved your life.
CRAIG: But it's a volunteer life squad. Volunteers don't go on strike.
EMILY: But if they did. If the ambu . . . if the life squad people were on strike. If I'd been chokin' to death and stopped breathin' and they were on strike, would you have saved me?
CRAIG: I don't know. I've never had the training for it.
MAN IN WHITE: Or much of anything else.
EMILY: But if you had.
CRAIG: Oh. Sure. If I'd known how, and you really were . . . of course.
EMILY: Thank you.
CRAIG: You're welcome.
MAN IN WHITE: Emily? Are you still mad at me? Is that why you're not speaking to me?
CRAIG: Is that what happens? Is that a spell? You just imagine somethin' happenin'?
EMILY: Of course.
CRAIG: Well, then, it's not like an actual spell or anything, is it?
EMILY: I'm not the one who called it a spell.
MAN IN WHITE: Please forgive me.
CRAIG: It's more like a flight of fancy.
EMILY: You make everything sound so poetic, Craig. I'd never have suspected it of you.
MAN IN WHITE: I'm the poetic one. Remember?
CRAIG: It was so weird. I mean I just stood there and all of a sudden, there was this whole other picture in my mind.

(Photo by Jan Deen)

EMILY: The . . . uh . . . height of the season, you say?

EMILY: You do understand, don't you.?
CRAIG: It's not always bad, though, is it? You can have good things happen, can't you?
EMILY: It depends on how cooperative the other characters are.
MAN IN WHITE: I'll be cooperative, Emily. Please don't ignore me like this. You know how sensitive and fragile I am.
CRAIG: I wonder if I can do it again?

[CRAIG *attempts to have a spell*]

MAN IN WHITE: This jerk doesn't seem to realize it takes years of practice to master the art, Emily. Why don't you just forget him and we'll run naked together through the blue grass.

[EMILY *considers this, looking at* CRAIG, *whose eyes are closed while having his spell. She seems to think he is the one who has just spoken.*]

EMILY: Yes.
MAN IN WHITE: With strawberries.
EMILY: Yes.
MAN IN WHITE: Yes.

[EMILY *kisses* CRAIG. MAN IN WHITE *notices.*]

MAN IN WHITE: No.
CRAIG: Oh!
EMILY: Oh!
MAN IN WHITE: Oh!
EMILY: I'm sorry. I just . . . it's the Kentucky sun. Yes. It gets to me sometimes. And as usual, I've made a fool of myself.
MAN IN WHITE: Non mi fa niente. Andiamo a vanga!
EMILY: I got carried away by my spell, even though it was really a flight of fancy. No wonder people make fun of me.
CRAIG: I wasn't making fun of you.
EMILY: I'm sorry. Truly. I'll just take my strawberries and be on my way to the bus stop.
MAN IN WHITE: Great!
EMILY: Oh, they're very nice, Craig. It's not every day you find strawberries like these.
CRAIG: Thank you.
EMILY: I bet you could learn to like them if you really tried. You were tempted, weren't you?
MAN IN WHITE: Hop on. We can just make it if we catch all the lights.
CRAIG: I'm allergic. Remember?
EMILY: That was before. Everything's changed now.
MAN IN WHITE: Didn't you learn anything from that last embarassing gaffe of yours? This guy and I are not, repeat, not, the same person.

He doesn't care about your strawberries and he doesn't care about you. You cannot continue to confuse us like this.
EMILY: [*To* CRAIG] You had a flight of fancy, remember?
MAN IN WHITE: Who cares?
EMILY: Come on. Try it. Just a little one.
MAN IN WHITE: Okay. Okay. Let's say he'll eat the strawberry. But what then? What happens at the end of the season?
EMILY and CRAIG: I don't know . . .
MAN IN WHITE: Remember the good old days? I'd feed you the strawberries one by one. Remember how I'd freeze them for the winter? And I'd let you lick them? This guy probably just swallows them whole.
EMILY: Just do it like I do. Real slow. Just run your tongue around the edges and then bite into it. Ever so gently. [*She demonstrates and is quite carried away by the experience.*]
MAN IN WHITE: Oh, yes.
CRAIG: You sure know how to handle a strawberry.
EMILY: Please. Try it now. I can't wait any longer.

[CRAIG *tentatively takes the strawberry, trying to follow her instructions. He is doing an adequate, if clumsy, job.* MAN IN WHITE, *however, also takes a strawberry and is handling it beautifully.* EMILY *is distracted by this and does not seem to notice* CRAIG *until he speaks.*]

CRAIG: I don't seem to be throwin' up.
EMILY: [*To* CRAIG] Oh, you did it. How nice.
CRAIG: Maybe I should have another. Just to be sure.
EMILY: They're quite addictive.
CRAIG: And delicious. I never used to care for 'em. Isn't that funny?
MAN IN WHITE: Hysterical.
CRAIG: This is incredible! I can see you!
MAN IN WHITE: Me? He sees me?
EMILY: Don't be ridiculous. He sees me.
MAN IN WHITE: So?
CRAIG: My eyes are closed and I can see you!
EMILY: Really?
CRAIG: I see you and a bicycle.
EMILY: Bicycle?
CRAIG: Yes! You're riding the bicycle past the stand here. You're screechin' to a halt. This is fantastic! I can really see it! You're gettin' off the bike and walkin' over to me . . .
EMILY: Would you mind terribly if I kissed you?
MAN IN WHITE: That's my line!
CRAIG: You're askin' me if you can kiss me.
EMILY: I've offended you. Please forgive me.

MAN IN WHITE: This is totally unfair, Emily.
CRAIG: No. No. You haven't offended me at all.
MAN IN WHITE: He's cheating!
CRAIG: You're wearin' this beautiful white dress. Its real low cut. And your hair is sort of sparkling in the sunlight. Gold, bronze, copper, silver. Even strawberry!
MAN IN WHITE: You're not falling for that?
EMILY: You know, Craig, I was thinking, maybe I won't go to Lexington today after all.
MAN IN WHITE: But you promised! The bus ride! We were going to lock ourselves in the bathroom.
EMILY: Instead, I might like to go on a picnic.
MAN IN WHITE: Ridiculous. You can't take the sun.
EMILY: A twilight picnic. With strawberries.
CRAIG: Sounds nice.
EMILY: Could I persuade you to join me?
CRAIG: Me?
EMILY: Do you see anyone else here I might be talking to?
CRAIG: Oh. Of course not.
MAN IN WHITE: If you go through with this, Emily. I shall have to withdraw my offer of the villa.
EMILY: The strawberry season is so short, you know, and I like to take advantage of it when I can.
CRAIG: It sounds wonderful.
EMILY: Really? You mean it?
CRAIG: I wouldn't say it if I didn't mean it.
MAN IN WHITE: One last chance before I pedal on to sunnier skies and bluer grass.
EMILY: Suit yourself.
MAN IN WHITE: I'm not kidding. I really mean it this time.
EMILY: So go.
MAN IN WHITE: You can't be serious.

[EMILY *ignores this and continues feeding strawberries to* CRAIG. MAN IN WHITE *is now pedaling his bicycle off stage.*]

EMILY: Drive carefully!
MAN IN WHITE: [*Exiting*] Two timing slut! Li mortacci tua! Va fa in cula! Schi fosa bruttacia!
EMILY: [*To* CRAIG] I don't suppose you speak any Italian?
CRAIG: Whatever for?
EMILY: Never mind. It's not important. Truly it isn't.

[*Lights fade*]

THE MEETING
(Louis B. Mayer Award Winner)

by

JEFF STETSON

Original Cast
(In Order of Appearance)

Rashad .... J. W. Smith
Malcolm X .... James Hawthorne
Dr. Martin Luther King, Jr. .... Jason Bernard

Directed by .... Shirley Jo Finney
Produced by .... Adam Leipzig & Diane White

Bill Bushnell, Artistic Producing Director

[*February 14, 1965.*]

A hotel room in Harlem.

It is the front room of a hotel suite. MALCOLM X *is asleep on the couch. The room is modestly furnished with a dresser with mirror, a television, night table, phone and lamp. There is a small study table with two straight-back chairs. There is a large window which overlooks all of Harlem. This window may be imaginary or real, and faces the audience.* MALCOLM X *is wearing a dark grey suit which is in need of an iron. His tie is loosened at the neck. This is a restless sleep that results in* MALCOLM *rising sharply and letting out a groan as if awakened by a nightmare.* RASHAD *enters quickly with a gun drawn. There is a tense moment as the two men look at each other.*]

MALCOLM: I just had a vision of America that nearly scared me to death, and now you come rushin' in here ready to kill me. Will you put that away.
RASHAD: [*Puts his gun back into his shoulder holster.*] What was it this time?
MALCOLM: [*Rises and begins to stretch.*] It doesn't matter. After a while they all start to seem the same.

[MALCOLM *looks at his watch.*]

He should be here soon.

[RASHAD *grunts his disapproval.*]

I take it you don't approve?

RASHAD: You know I don't. But since when has that made a difference?
MALCOLM: [*Looks at* RASHAD *and smiles gently.*] Stop pouting.
RASHAD: Malcolm, why are you meeting with him?

[*Pause.*]

MALCOLM: Do you remember the first time you made love?
RASHAD: What?
MALCOLM: Do you remember the first time you made love?
RASHAD: Yeah, sort of.
MALCOLM: Why did you do it?
RASHAD: What do you mean, why did I do it?
MALCOLM: Was it planned? Was there a reason behind it? Or did it just happen because it was meant to? Because you knew sooner or later you would . . . because it was time.
RASHAD: [*Thinks for a moment.*] It was mostly 'cause the woman said I could.

MALCOLM: [*Laughs and shakes his head.*] Rashad, there's nothing romantic about you. If you weren't my bodyguard, I think you'd be alone.

RASHAD: For all you share with me, sometimes I am.

MALCOLM: [*Walks to the dresser and studies himself in the mirror.*] Did I ever tell you about Billie Holiday? She sang a song for me once, you know. Did I ever tell you that?

[MALCOLM *moves toward* RASHAD.]

She took the flower out of her hair and gave it to me. Then she sang.

[MALCOLM *thinks about the moment, after a pause begins to sing softly.*]

"YOU DON'T KNOW WHAT LOVE IS
UNTIL YOU'VE LEARNED THE MEANING OF THE BLUES
UNTIL YOU'VE LOVED A LOVE YOU'VE HAD TO LOSE
YOU DON'T KNOW WHAT LOVE IS"

[MALCOLM *is swaying back and forth.* RASHAD *after listening begins to move a bit himself, until he finds himself doing a slow dance and joins* MALCOLM *for the second verse.*]

BOTH: "YOU DON'T KNOW HOW HEARTS YEARN
FOR LOVE THAT CANNOT LIVE YET NEVER DIES"

[*On the word "dies",* MALCOLM *seems to become sullen, lost in thought. He goes through with the rest of the song, but there is no movement or life in contrast to* RASHAD *who is now lost in the song and loving it.*]

"UNTIL YOU'VE FACED EACH DAWN WITH
SLEEPLESS EYES
YOU DON'T KNOW WHAT LOVE IS."

[RASHAD *becomes aware of the mood change and looks at* MALCOLM *who has turned and after several moments seems to notice the phone and is drawn to it. He takes the phone, dials it, and waits.*]

MALCOLM: Hi, it's me . . . Are you okay? . . . And the children? [*He smiles, but it is a smile with more than a trace of concern.*]

They always could sleep through anything . . . Just like their mama. . . .

[*There is a quiet, painful laugh.*]

Betty? . . . I'm sorry for not being there with you. You know that, don't you? . . . Next week, when I speak at the Audubon, I want you there with me. I want the whole family there. After that, we'll spend more time together. I promise . . . Don't get so excited girl, we got enough children. [*He laughs. It seems more relaxed.*] I've got to go, he should be here soon . . . Betty? . . . I love you. [*The words come out slowly, and painfully real.*] Kiss the children for me, and if you've been good you can also give yourself a big hug.

[MALCOLM *smiles, and it gradually turns to the word, "Good-bye". He cradles the phone for several moments, then places it softly in its rightful place. He bows his head slightly and quickly pounds his fist into the palm of his hand. He does this only once, and it seems to release the tension, at least, momentarily. He begins to relax and picks up the phone again.* RASHAD *has been the loyal observer during all of this, wishing to give his friend privacy yet there to help at the first sign.* MALCOLM *speaks into the phone again.*]

If the F.B.I. is still listening, I'm hungry . . . could you deliver some Chinese food and red soda?

[*He starts to hang up, then remembers.*]

Oh . . . and hold the pork.

[*Both* MALCOLM *and* RASHAD *look at each other and laugh. After several moments,* RASHAD *walks toward* MALCOLM.]

RASHAD: Is everything all right?
MALCOLM: [*Nods yes.*] The children are asleep.
RASHAD: Sister Betty?
MALCOLM: [*There is a painful, bittersweet pause.*] Our house is bombed this morning, and I'm here . . . I haven't given her much have I, Rashad?
RASHAD: Do you think she would ever feel that?
MALCOLM: She would never be that selfish. But I know. I can hear it in her voice, the fear, for me mostly, but for the family too. I should be with her tonight. I should be with my children as often as possible.

[*Pause.*]

They should remember their daddy.
RASHAD: The *world* will remember their daddy.
MALCOLM: I won't be remembered. I know that. If I could just be sure that what I represent will be remembered. That's all that's important to me. This country will do what it can to see that that won't happen.
RASHAD: This country has always tried its best to eliminate the black man. It ain't happened yet.
MALCOLM: What can be changed, doesn't need to be eliminated.

[MALCOLM *takes his glasses off, rubs the bridge of his nose, gently.*]

I'm tired, Rashad . . . It seems like I've been a lot of things lately . . . but whatever else I've been . . . tired has been in there somewhere.

[*Pause.*]

It's stuffy in here.

[MALCOLM *moves toward the window but* RASHAD *rushes to stop him.*]

RASHAD: Stay away from the window, Malcolm! Please.

[MALCOLM *moves back toward the seat, but remains standing.* RASHAD *cautiously opens the window, making sure that the curtain remains drawn.*]

MALCOLM: All the forces in this country couldn't protect their own President. You think it makes a difference not to be able to breathe the Harlem air?
RASHAD: It may make a difference *tonight*.
MALCOLM: Those used to be my streets, Rashad.
RASHAD: They'll always be your streets . . . They'll just never be safe.

[*Pause.*]

Just give the word, MALCOLM and we can strike back.
MALCOLM: [*Angrily.*] Strike back? Do you think I trained them in the art of self defense, so they could protect themselves from *us*?
RASHAD: Did you train them to throw a fire-bomb through your window?
MALCOLM: [*Moves slowly toward* RASHAD.] I don't think it was them.
RASHAD: [*Frustrated.*] Malcolm!
MALCOLM: No, Rashad. It just doesn't make any sense. Even Elijah doesn't have the power to do some of the things that's happened recently.

[*Pause.*]

It's gone way beyond that. Next Sunday, at the rally, I'm going to say some things, some things that might really begin to put the heat on us . . . I'm going to say that it's not the Muslims.
RASHAD: And who are you going to accuse?
MALCOLM: Who else could it be? Do you think Elijah could get the French government to ban me from France?
RASHAD: You won't ever get the letters out of your mouth, Malcolm.
MALCOLM: [*Smiles.*] I'll just have to remember to talk fast.
RASHAD: We can't afford to lose you.
MALCOLM: When I can't even afford to go near that window, you already have.
RASHAD: Won't you at least cut back on some of the speaking engagements? There's no way we can manage large crowds anymore. Not when we have to watch out for people who look like *us*.
MALCOLM: Ain't no one out on those streets look like you, Rashad.

You got to go *clear* 'cross the ocean, to another land, to find someone as *ugly* as you. Either that, or all the way downtown.

[*Both men laugh.*]

RASHAD: Please be serious, Malcolm. . . .
MALCOLM: [*Smiles.*] After the Audubon, I'll cut down. Anyway, I told Sister Betty I would be with her more often. It's the first time she laughed in months.

[MALCOLM *looks at his watch again. He senses* RASHAD's *concern.*]

He should be here by now.
RASHAD: [*Places hand gently on* MALCOLM's *arm.*] Can you trust him?

[MALCOLM *smiles, reassuringly touches* RASHAD's *hand, then walks away slowly.*]

Well, it's a good thing you're meeting him in a hotel room.

[MALCOLM *turns toward* RASHAD, *for an explanation.*]

If it gets dull, you can always give him a Bible to read.

[MALCOLM *laughs and is interrupted by a knock at the door. He looks at* RASHAD *for several moments, then speaks.*]

MALCOLM: Don't you think you ought to let him in?
RASHAD: You know what I think.

[RASHAD *goes to the door and opens it. He greets* DR. KING *who enters, holding a small brown bag. He looks at* MALCOLM.]

DR. KING: Malcolm.
MALCOLM: Doctor King.

[*Pause.*]

Rashad, I think you can leave Doctor King and I together. We'll be all right.
MALCOLM: [*Pauses, uncomfortably.*] I need to check Doctor King.
DR. KING: Check? I was "checked" once downstairs.
RASHAD: Not by me.
MALCOLM: [*Smiles.*] Rashad, somehow I think that's unnecessary. I'm sure I'll be safe with Doctor King.
RASHAD: I'm sure you'd be safe with Doctor King, too, but how do I know that's him?
DR. KING: Perhaps I could give a short speech, or an appropriate sermon.
MALCOLM: Oh please, Doctor, not that.

[*Both men laugh good-naturedly.*]

We'll be okay, Rashad.

RASHAD: Very well, I'll be just outside, if you need me.

[*Pause.*]

Can I take your coat, Doctor?

DR. KING: Why, thank you.

[RASHAD *helps* DR. KING *off with his coat, and manages to get a quick, but obvious frisk or two in as well.* MALCOLM *gives an embarrassed glance toward* DR. KING. RASHAD *exits having accomplished what he set out to do, and is satisfied about having done it.*]

MALCOLM: I'm sorry about that . . . these are troubled times.

DR. KING: I understand . . . I suppose the bombing has unsettled everyone.

MALCOLM: [*Smiles.*] Didn't do much for the price of real estate in my neighborhood . . . I was thinking of adding a room anyway . . Did anyone see you come in?

DR. KING: No. I followed your instructions. The next time you want me to take the back stairs, I wish you could get a room on a floor lower than the seventh.

MALCOLM: [*Laughs.*] I've seen you on T.V. You could afford to lose a few pounds.

DR. KING: Television makes you look heavier . . . And, anyway, this stomach is in the finest sense of southern tradition and the ministry. Congregations don't warm up to thin preachers . . . means the preachin's not good enough to receive sweet potato pies in lieu of other donations.

MALCOLM: My congregation sells pies street to street . . . You might say it keeps them thin and the donations fat. [*Looks at the bag.*] Speaking of pies, is that your lunch in that bag . . . or perhaps a tape recorder?

DR. KING: And why would I need a tape recorder?

MALCOLM: Maybe you're nervous about coming out of hotel rooms . . . Mister Hoover does have a way of making persons paranoid.

DR. KING: I have never thought that the Lord could have made a mistake . . . but Hoover does push one's faith beyond reasonable limits.

MALCOLM: Have a seat, Reverend.

[DR. KING *places the bag on the couch, and takes a seat near the table.*]

MALCOLM: Don't you want the couch?

DR. KING: I don't want to get too comfortable.

MALCOLM: Oh, yes . . . I forgot; you're used to sit-ins and such.

DR. KING: I find they're generally better for your back.

MALCOLM: Not too good for the head, as I recall. I'm surprised you still have one with all that nonviolent *action* you've been involved in.

DR. KING: You'd be amazed how much one can take, when the purpose is clear.
MALCOLM: Perhaps, but I think some folks just naturally have hard heads.

[MALCOLM *takes his seat, directly across the table from* DR. KING.]

When I was in Selma two weeks ago, I was tempted to come by and pay you a visit.
DR. KING: You should have; plenty of room in the jail.
MALCOLM: I try not to visit jails, voluntarily.
DR. KING: I heard your speech on my behalf was very moving.
MALCOLM: The *younger* people seemed to enjoy it. In fact, if I had spoken any longer, we all would have come by the jailhouse . . . except we wouldn't be planning on stayin'. . . of course, there probably wouldn't have been much jail remainin' after we left.
DR. KING: Then, I should thank you for not speaking too long. Being in jail is unpleasant enough . . . having it torn down while you're there is not my idea of how to spend a Sunday afternoon.
MALCOLM: Oh, you can thank some of your conference planners for that. If it were up to them, I wouldn't have spoken at all. As it was, they spent several hours after I spoke trying to calm the crowd down.
DR. KING: Maybe they were trying to move them in a different direction.
MALCOLM: Calming them down certainly would have done that.
DR. KING: Well, since you didn't visit me then, I'm visiting you now.
MALCOLM: Yes, and I must say, I'm impressed. I didn't think you visited Northern cities too often. I imagine our streets are more difficult to maneuver than those country roads you're accustomed to.
DR. KING: If the road was meant to be traveled, it will be.
MALCOLM: And if it's destroyed?
DR. KING: It will be rebuilt. Or it wasn't the road for us.
MALCOLM: Still the dreamer?
DR. KING: And you're still the revolutionary?
MALCOLM: [*Smiles.*] Thank you.
DR. KING: I hadn't realized I had paid you a compliment.
MALCOLM: Ignorance is sometimes the sincerest form of flattery.
DR. KING: If I didn't know better, I'd think you were trying to upset me.
MALCOLM: [*Smiles.*] A man that allows himself to get hit upside the head, certainly wouldn't get upset at mere words.

[MALCOLM *moves toward the dresser and takes an apple from a fruit basket. He brings it toward* DR. KING.]

I want you to eat this.
DR. KING: No, thank you . . . I'm not hungry.
MALCOLM: I don't care . . . I want you to eat it anyway.

DR. KING: I don't want it.
MALCOLM: It's good for you.
DR. KING: That may be, but I still don't want it.
MALCOLM: What if I make you eat it?
DR. KING: And just how would you do that?
MALCOLM: By force, if necessary.
DR. KING: I'd still refuse.
MALCOLM: You mean to tell me, you would refuse to eat this apple, even if I resorted to force?
DR. KING: Yes.
MALCOLM: Even if it's good for you?
DR. KING: Even then.

[MALCOLM *smiles, takes a bite of the apple, and chews very slowly.*]

MALCOLM: You're right, Martin. You can't force people to take something they don't want. Try as hard as you can to make white folks love us, no matter how smooth you make it, the simple fact is, they just won't swallow the truth . . . even if it's good for them.

[*The two men look at each other in silence for a moment.*]

DR. KING: Isn't it odd, that you should tempt me with an apple?
MALCOLM: [*Smiles.*] You see the apple as a temptation . . . I see it as nourishment.
DR. KING: We see what we want to see, I suppose.
MALCOLM: Some of us don't see anything at all, even when it's staring right at us. For example, when you entered the front of the hotel, did you notice a woman standing outside? She was wearing a short red dress and heavy makeup.
DR. KING: The prostitute?
MALCOLM: [*Nods yes.*] How old would you guess she is?
DR. KING: Thirty to thirty-five?
MALCOLM: [*A painful laugh.*] She's seventeen, Reverend. Although after three years on the street, age has no real significance. Tomorrow morning she won't know how many men she slept with tonight . . . let alone in the last month . . . in the last year. She can't even tell from the money she makes. Her pimp collects that right after each trick.

[MALCOLM *stands and moves slowly across the room.*]

She's part of a larger congregation, but you won't find them in any of your churches. They would curse your God if they were alive enough to curse. But they're dead, Martin. They're the living dead. They exist because they're accustomed to it and haven't thought about why they shouldn't. If they weren't used to moving so

often . . . not staying in any one place too long . . . someone would have swept them away by now.
DR. KING: I take it you have a point to all this?
MALCOLM: I know something of the living dead, young women working the streets, and their pimps. When you're around the same people every day, you don't notice the change right away. Then all of a sudden, you're aware . . . someone is fat or old . . . or without hope. The purpose of all this, Martin . . . is to show you the hopeless and to let you know that the number is growing every day.
DR. KING: Do you have a solution?
MALCOLM: Unity.
DR. KING: I've never been against that.
MALCOLM: Your unity is sitting around the campfire while the cross is burning, singing "We shall overcome." If you're really for unity you'd be singing, "We shall come over!" Every time there's an injustice, we shall come over. Every time there's a black woman being frightened by a white face behind a white hood, we shall come over. Every time and *anytime* there's a need to stop white people from persecuting black people, WE SHALL COME OVER! And we will stay until black people feel safe again.
DR. KING: Violence? Revenge? Is that the unity you seek?
MALCOLM: I care about survival Martin. I care about the quality of that survival. No. I don't seek violence. I seek to stop it and I'll stop it in whatever way I can. I have that as a duty.
DR. KING: Violence never stops violence, Malcolm.
MALCOLM: But marches do? All those people gathered together singing songs. What did that bring? A piece of legislation? Did that legislation help those civil rights workers killed in the South . . . or the children blown-up in their own church? You got nothing, Martin! never happened. The little progress we thought had been made was all but eliminated, or else used in such a way as to undermine its Nothing . . . but some more empty promises, and a piece of paper that betrayed yet another lie in a long list of lies . . . the American lie . . . the grand *white* lie.

[*Pause.*]

You know, I had a dream last night.
DR. KING: Oh?
MALCOLM: [*Smiles.*] I'm sorry, that's your line.
DR. KING: You may borrow it, if you choose.
MALCOLM: This dream I had . . . we had been dead for some time . . . the time it takes to mis-educate the average American. Young black men and women didn't know who we were. They knew nothing about the movement . . . the struggle. It was like it had

never happened. The little progress we thought had been made was all but eliminated, or else used in such a way as to undermine its original purpose. I woke up in a cold sweat, shaking, confused. You know, Martin, I have seen my own death countless nights, but that vision was never as frightening as that dream.

[*Pause.*]

We will be sold out . . . you and I. It might happen over a promise for a job . . . or a deal to be supported as the new leader. It might even happen over a basketball scholarship. It may happen any number of ways . . . but it will happen, Martin. You might even do it to yourself.

DR. KING: And how do you think I will accomplish my own undermining?

[MALCOLM *takes a piece of paper from the inside of his jacket. He unfolds it neatly and begins to read, at first, seriously, then a bit mockingly, then finally, with some degree of anger.*]

MALCOLM: "We will match your capacity to inflict suffering, with our capacity to endure it. We will meet your physical force with soul force. Do to us what you will. Threaten our children and we will *still* love you. Come into our homes at the midnight hour of life, take us out on some desolate highway and *beat us* and then leave us there and we will *still love you.* Say that we aren't worthy of integration; that we are too *immoral;* that we are too *low;* that we are too *degraded* and we will still love you. Bomb our homes and go by our churches early in the morning and bomb them if you please . . . and we will still love you.

[MALCOLM *slides the paper toward* DR. KING.]

We will wear you down, with *our* capacity to *suffer!"*

[*Pause.*]

Did you really say that, Martin?
DR. KING: You know I said it. And, furthermore, you know the context.
MALCOLM: The context! The context has to be insanity!
DR. KING: Is love insane?
MALCOLM: No! But we aren't talking about love.
DR. KING: Maybe you need to read it again.
MALCOLM: I try not to inflict suffering on myself more than once. I suppose my *capacity* for that is not as large as yours.
DR. KING: [*Leans forward, angrily.*] You are not before any cameras now Malcolm! You have an audience of one, and I am not cheering. So, you can stop with the sarcasm and your flippant remarks!
MALCOLM: I don't want any cameras and I don't need any audience!

DR. KING: And I didn't come here to debate you, so you can stop the contest.

MALCOLM: The *contest* is more important than a debate, Doctor!

[*Both men are leaning toward each other. Their opposite arms are extended, elbows on the table, coming to rest in an arm-wrestling position. Their hands touch, by accident or impulse, and they both smile. At first the smile appears to be a sly one, then it turns to a satisfying grin, as they seem to fall naturally into an arm-wrestling contest. They struggle briefly, but not strenuously.* MALCOLM *wins and the two men stare at each other silently, for several moments.*]

DR. KING: [MALCOLM *still has* DR. KING's *arm pinned to the table, but without force.*] Are you satisfied?

MALCOLM: [*Letting* DR. KING's *hand go.*] I wish it were that easy, Doctor.

DR. KING: Why is it that every time you say the words "Doctor" or "Reverend" I have the distinct impression I should feel insulted?

MALCOLM: [*Laughs.*] I imagine it's my street accent. Having not had the advantage of university training . . . my words sometimes appear too harsh.

DR. KING: But you lectured at a fairly prestigious university as I recall.

MALCOLM: There are universities, and then of course, there's Harvard. They didn't bring me there to lecture. They brought me there to be embarrassed. But then I don't embarrass easily. And since Harvard didn't have anything I wanted . . . I never saw a reason to apologize for not having it. Of course, there were an ample number of Negroes there who seemed to have an abundance of apologies all saved up for just such an occasion.

DR. KING: Do you see me as that kind of Negro?

MALCOLM: No. But I see you being used by white folks, whether you intend to be or not. Which is why they'll erect monuments to you before you're through.

DR. KING: Oh, I don't know about that. Seems like the mention of your name is likely to cause a great deal of attention. They may even name whole cities after you.

MALCOLM: You got the award, Martin.

DR. KING: Yes. On behalf of all of us. People everywhere who fought against injustice.

MALCOLM: White people gave you the award, Martin. Doesn't it worry you just a little that the people who are doing most of the oppressing are also giving out all the awards? I think you must have impressed them most when you said, "If blood has to flow on the streets . . . let it be ours." Hell, every cracker in the South would have chipped in to buy you an award for that one!

DR. KING: The award was for *peace*, Malcolm.

MALCOLM: No, Doctor, the award was for getting beaten and not fighting back.

DR. KING: I didn't expect acceptance from you, Malcolm. A little understanding would be sufficient.

MALCOLM: You want me to understand how a black man would ask his people to be the first, last, and only ones to bleed? To give their precious blood, let it spill to the pavements of these cities, or sink into the soil of this nation, the nation we helped build? You want me to *understand* that?

DR. KING: Did it ever occur to you that perhaps you were more responsible for the blood of our people flowing than I? That your speeches are unwittingly causing violence?

MALCOLM: No! Not once! Not ever! Aggression in the name of self-defense is not violence. It's honor. We have to begin to *think* for ourselves. To *do* for ourselves. Not let the "man" shape our values for us; 'cause he has some tricky logic. He'll make us think that defending our families is wrong. That defending our communities is violence. When the music is a tango . . . you tango. Simple as that. If they don't want you to tango, stop playin' the music and then maybe we can waltz . . . nice and polite like, with white gloves and black ties.

DR. KING: Don't you think we've made any progress, Malcolm

MALCOLM: Progress? Martin, you got some concessions because I was the alternative. They threw some legislation, some money, and some cracker-controlled programs your way in hopes that nonviolence would win out. Only we were the ones to remain nonviolent.

[*Pause.*]

If they kill me first, you'll have nothing to negotiate with. If they kill you first, they can't let me live. They'll make you into a martyr, Martin. They'll hold your nonviolent methods up to the world as a testament to your courage. If they hold it up long enough, people won't even notice the contradiction; you were *killed* preaching it. We can't learn anything from martyrs anymore, Martin.

DR. KING: Jesus was a martyr.

MALCOLM: Two thousand ago it was possible to die and not kill a movement. Today it's brought to you in living color . . . flashed across the big screen and the small, all with the same clear and unrelenting message, "when you lead, you die." How long will we continue teaching that to our children?

[DR. KING *walks toward the window and stares outside.* MALCOLM, *who is now seated, looks silently at the floor. He looks toward* DR. KING, *and begins to speak again.*]

The Meeting

This ain't the country, Reverend. They stack families on top of each other out here . . . black man on top of black man . . . .'til there's no room . . . . 'til you can't breathe. When you can't breathe you either die, or you strike out and someone else dies. The women, the only time they have a chance to lie down is when they're working. And then, Martin, there's the drugs. You put enough drugs out there, and they'll dream anything. Why, they'll even believe your dreams, Doctor.

DR. KING: I can't change, Malcolm. I think you know that.

MALCOLM: Everyone can change. That girl in the street changed. Three years ago, she was fourteen, today she. . .

DR. KING: I *can't* change!

[MALCOLM *takes his glasses off, massages the bridge of his nose and gradually his temple. He puts his glasses back on and looks at* DR. KING, *who has turned away from the window, and moves back toward his seat.*]

[*Softly.*] Neither can you.

MALCOLM: If you can't change, can you at least get angry?

DR. KING: [*Smiles, gradually turning to some distant recollection.*] The first time I ever led a march . . . I remember being surrounded by all kinds of people. Old women, who found it hard to walk across the room, somehow found strength to march for miles. Young men and women carrying their children. Older children holding the hands of their younger brothers and sisters. All of a sudden a bottle was thrown from the middle of a crowd of whites. We shouted "duck!" And all the adults did. But children . . . children have a need to know what's being done. The bottle struck this young child. It cut the whole left side of her face. None of us really had time to be angry then. We rushed to protect her . . . to console her . . . to worry about stopping the bleeding. But we marched on.

[DR. KING *is speaking with a sense of emotion that makes* MALCOLM *realize he is reliving that moment, with all the pain and fear that must have existed.*]

Then, a few moments later, this huge white man . . . bigger than the truck he must have been driving that night . . . this man with all his force yelled: "Go home you little NIGGER BASTARD!" He was screaming at this young boy, couldn't have been older than seven or eight.

[*Pause.*]

I saw the look on this child's face. He was scared . . . and hurt, and maybe most of all, ashamed. He thought he must have done something terribly wrong to have all that hate directed toward him.

DR. KING: I'm willing to call it a draw if you are.
MALCOLM: Okay, you stop first.

[*Looking directly at* MALCOLM.]

Yes, Malcolm, I can get angry . . . with all the history that makes me a black man . . . I can get angry. But it's a different kind of anger, an anger that makes you know you can't stop lovin' . . . can't stop believin'. It's an anger that makes you want to prove hate wrong.
MALCOLM: Prove hate wrong? [*Smiles.*] I just want to prove it less powerful.
DR. KING: We both deal with power, Malcolm. We just do it differently.
MALCOLM: Yes. You see our children bleeding and in tears and you seek to comfort them. I see the man who has the rock in his hand and I seek to stop him. If I can't stop him before he throws it, I'll see to it that he never throws another.
DR. KING: And what will that accomplish, Malcolm? If you stop that one, there will just be another, and another, and another.
MALCOLM: Doctor, it doesn't matter how good a football player you are, when the game is baseball you better get yourself a bat. And if you've got problems swinging it, you ought to stay out of the game.
DR. KING: Somehow, I had hoped that the game had changed. Your trips abroad seemed to have given you a great vision . . . a broader compassion.
MALCOLM: You don't tame the lion and leave the jungle unchanged

Martin. Yes. I saw things outside this country, saw things that perhaps my heart wouldn't or couldn't let me see before. I saw whites, who when they talked about color, made it seem incidental; like describing a suit or a sunset. But here, [*Smiles.*] here, it's different. When the "Man" here talks about color, you know what he means. You hear it in his voice, see it in his expression. He means he's on top and you're not. And there's no way he's gonna let that change. It's a simple question of power and privilege. And the one in power, always decides the privilege.

[*He touches* DR. KING's *arm slightly.*]

We aren't the ones in power, Martin. And we won't be until we gain control of our own lives, our own thinking.

DR. KING: You want to free blacks. I want to free America. It's the only way any of us can be free, Malcolm.

MALCOLM: [*Frustrated.*] Martin, can't you see what's happening to us? Five years from now, ten at the most, whites won't have to do anything to us. We'll be doing it to ourselves. Some of the brothers who sit peacefully in your demonstrations, and have their heads split open, do you know they go back to their *own* communities and commit violent acts. It's the *rage*, Martin. It's the *hurt* that's all balled up inside and makes you strike out in the only way you can . . . the only way that's acceptable.

[*Pause.*]

I can't free us from that rage . . . but at least I can try and direct it to the right source.

DR. KING: Don't we really want the same things, Malcolm?

MALCOLM: You want us to be able to buy a cup of coffee. I want us to be able to sell it. You want us to integrate the coffee shop. I want us to own it. You want white folks to hire us. I want us to be able to hire ourselves. No, Martin, we do not want the same things. I'm afraid your quest for integration will be the white man's solution for control. Maybe the only hope he have is that they'll hate us so much that they won't recognize the power they'd have if they let us in.

DR. KING: And so, those of us who don't agree with your definition of power and control . . . I suppose we are to be called, "Uncle Toms?"

MALCOLM: I only refer to the *older* ones as "Uncle". . . and I don't call them "Tom" anymore. I call them "Roy" or "Ralph" or "Uncle Whitney."

DR. KING: They don't deserve that from you, Malcolm. They don't deserve that from anyone. Do you think the unity you seek can be achieved through insult and ridicule?

MALCOLM: [*Innocently.*] Have I "ridiculed" you, Reverend?
DR. KING: Did you think I should be flattered at the term "Reverend Doctor Chickenleg?"
MALCOLM: Oh, so there *is* an ego to bruise. And it was "Chickenwing" to be more precise. Would you have found it more flattering if I referred to you as "De Lawd?"
DR. KING: [DR. KING *begins to roll up his sleeve.*] "The Movement" would have been sufficient.
MALCOLM: [*Smiles, while taking his jacket off.*] Isn't it wonderful how well the two of us are getting along?
DR. KING: I suppose it's time for a rematch?
MALCOLM: You should feel fortunate that a rematch is possible. Oh well, my friend, I am prepared to inflict suffering if you are prepared to endure it.

[*Both men smile. It's a smile less sly and more respectful than the first contest, but still manifesting a degree of distance. After a brisk encounter,* DR. KING *emerges the winner.*]

Well, it seems we are even, Reverend.
DR. KING: Yes. I suppose we are. Is that why you invited me?
MALCOLM: Actually, I'm surprised you accepted the invitation.
DR. KING: I came because I wanted to offer my protection.
MALCOLM: [*In disbelief.*] What?
DR. KING: When I heard about this morning, I thought you . . .
MALCOLM: [*Laughs.*] Protection? You? Offer me . . . protection? [*Angrily.*] And how are you going to do that, sir. Are you going to have a mass sit-in . . . try to diffuse the bombs by praying for a heavy wind that might blow out the fire! Or perhaps your nonviolent *action* movement will frighten the Molotov cocktail throwers so much that . . .
DR. KING: [*Angrily.*] Molotov cocktails are part of *your* movement, Malcolm, not mine!
MALCOLM: Yes, Doctor King, *my* movement is *flexible*. It considers *all* options! It rules *nothing* out! Its one goal is *freedom*. Absolute. Total. And complete. It doesn't ask. It takes. It's willing to pay the price for freedom. Those that aren't willing to pay for it really don't want it.
DR. KING: Don't set yourself up as the authority on freedom, Malcolm!
MALCOLM: Why, I wouldn't think of it, Reverend. "Authorities" are those who study so hard to be white. If they do real good, they get to be "scholars" and if they speak for all Negroes, they get to be called "authorities"!
DR. KING: I came here to offer my help, Malcolm. If you don't want it I can . . .
MALCOLM: Your help? You're helping to kill me, Doctor!

DR. KING: Am I to be accused of that too?
MALCOLM: Not accused. Indicted! The cost for black people fighting each other is death, Martin. When we are divided, we are destroyed. It not only becomes easy for white people to kill us, it becomes justifiable.
DR. KING: And you think I've contributed to that?
MALCOLM: Let's just say, anyone who wants to kill me, anyone who wants to kill any black man, does not have to stop and think about the consequences of their actions. They don't stop to ask: "Now, what would the good Doctor, do?" They know what you'll do. Nothing!
DR. KING: Don't mistake nonviolence for non-action, Malcolm. You do a disservice to those who have been beaten so that you might have the freedom to question their courage.
MALCOLM: I have never questioned their courage, just their judgment.
DR. KING: I'm beginning to question my own for coming here.
MALCOLM: Well, that can be easily corrected, Doctor. The same steps that brought you here, will lead you away.
DR. KING: On that, we can at least agree. [*Gets his hat and coat.*] Thanks for the lecture on unity.
MALCOLM: You're welcome. And before you go, you should know this: my faith teaches me not to embarrass even my own enemies. I let you beat me in arm wrestling the second time.
DR. KING: My faith teaches me to show mercy, especially to my enemies. I let you beat me the first time. It seemed the Christian thing to do.

[DR. KING *begins to move toward the door as* MALCOLM *spots the paper bag and picks it up.*]

MALCOLM: You forgot your lunch.
DR. KING: It's not mine. It's a gift.

[MALCOLM *opens the bag and removes a black doll. He looks at it suspiciously and then says sarcastically:*]

MALCOLM: Is this what you brought me for protection? Does it possess some kind of magical powers? Or is the doll nonviolent too?
DR. KING: It's not for you. It's for your daughter. My family was watching television when the news bulletin about the bombing appeared. They showed a film report of the damage to your home. You were on the front lawn holding one of your daughters.
MALCOLM: [*Softly.*] Attallah?
DR. KING: Yes. My daughter wondered if everything in the house had been destroyed. When she learned that I was going to see you tonight she thought Attallah could use a friend. That's her favorite doll. If it has any "magical powers" I suppose it's because of that.
MALCOLM: [*For the first time, he is unsure and obviously taken aback*

by the kindness as well as by his own actions.] I . . . What's her name?
DR. KING: I don't know that she has one.
MALCOLM: [*Smiles.*] I meant your daughter's.
DR. KING: [*Chuckles.*] Yolanda.
MALCOLM: How old is she?
DR. KING: Nine.
MALCOLM: Attallah is six. She will love this, very much.

[*Pause.*]

Thank your daughter, thank, Yolanda, for her . . . for both of us.

[*The two men stare at each other briefly, somewhat awkwardly and yet with a sense of tenderness brought on by the moment.* DR. KING *nods approval or possibly goodbye as he turns to exit.* MALCOLM *quickly and loudly says:*]

Doctor King! . . .

[*There is a pause as the two men face each other again.*]

I suppose we ought to declare a winner.
DR. KING: [*Smiles.*] Yes . . . I suppose we should. If there can't be a truce at least there ought to be a winner.

[*Both men move toward the table, position themselves for the final contest, and loosen their ties and shirts for maximum comfort.*]

MALCOLM: Don't take advantage of me, Reverend. Remember I'm older than you.
DR. KING: The public for some reason continues to think of you as younger.
MALCOLM: They associate militancy [*Spits in his hand.*] with youthfulness.
DR. KING: That's odd, it's rather an [*Spits in his hands.*] old idea.

[*They both lock hands.*]

MALCOLM: Some of the best ideas are.
DR. KING: Whoever wins in here will not necessarily be the winner outside you know?
MALCOLM: If I thought that, *I* would have invited you, a long time ago.

[*Both men are now seriously into the combat.* MALCOLM *begins to get a slight advantage.*]

Beware, Doctor. The old man is taking charge.
DR. KING: [*Begins to even the contest.*] "HE didn't lead me here only to have me turn around now!"

MALCOLM: Quoting Scriptures won't help you.

[*Both men are seesawing to victory.*]

DR. KING: [*Straining a bit.*] Can't hurt.

MALCOLM: You should fight this hard when some sheriff tries to put a knot upside your head.

DR. KING: I fight even harder then. You just haven't noticed.

[*Pause.*]

I'm willing to call it a draw if you are.

MALCOLM: Okay, you stop first.

DR. KING: I'm from the country, Malcolm, but give me some credit.

MALCOLM: All right . . . All right . . . I'll count to three.

DR. KING: Are you going to do all the counting?

MALCOLM: [*Still struggling.*] We'll alternate. Does that meet with your approval?

DR. KING: They taught me at school that "three" was an odd number.

MALCOLM: I'll start, you go next, and we'll finish at the same time. Agreed?

DR. KING: Agreed.

MALCOLM: One.

DR. KING: Two.

BOTH: Three.

[*They both stop and let out groans of battle. They look at their hands which have taken much punishment.*]

DR. KING: If we had joined hands and pushed in the same direction, just imagine what we could have accomplished.

[DR. KING *starts to laugh quietly. He then shakes his head in disbelief.*]

MALCOLM: Something funny?

DR. KING: I was just thinking about what Coretta would say, if she knew you and I spent the night arm wrestling.

[*There is a pause as the two men look at each other in silence. It is a tender look, a look of concern and admiration.*]

MALCOLM: [*Softly*] Your children? Your family? Do you ever wonder what would happen to them, if you weren't around anymore?

DR. KING: Only every morning. And then again before I go to bed.

MALCOLM: And it doesn't make a difference, does it?

DR. KING: It always makes a difference. It just doesn't change anything.

MALCOLM: It's ironic, you tried to stop whites from hating us and I tried to stop us from hating ourselves. We'll probably be killed by those who we tried so hard to teach.

DR. KING: What makes you think that a black will kill you?

MALCOLM: There won't be any whites who could get close enough. I just hope it happens from someone I don't know. I would hate to think I could be that wrong about a friend.
DR. KING: Could we have been friends, Malcolm?

[*Pause.*]

MALCOLM: If we had time, perhaps. [*Beat.*] If only we had time.
DR. KING: Why did you really want to see me, Malcolm?
MALCOLM: [*Softly.*] I don't know. I suppose I wanted to see if you'd come.
DR. KING: Another test?
MALCOLM: No. Another chance.

[*Pause.*]

Did you really come here to offer protection?
DR. KING: Maybe I should have said, comfort . . . the type of comfort one man can give to another.
MALCOLM: Do you think that people will remember us as "men" and only "men?"
DR. KING: No. And we can't afford to let them know that that's all we are. At least, not for awhile.
MALCOLM: I wonder what type of men we would have been had we been born in a different time. A time when race didn't matter, when injustice was just a part of a history lesson.
DR. KING: I imagine we would have been quite dull.
MALCOLM: [*Laughs.*] And we would have grown very old.
DR. KING: The dull have a way of outliving the rest of us. Perhaps that's their greatest punishment.
MALCOLM: Punishment? . . . I saw my father killed because he spoke out. I institutionalized my own mother because some pain deep inside of her drowned out the language of the world. I have nothing to leave my own family, not even a home. And yet, I still wonder, was there more I should have done . . . more of myself I could have given?
DR. KING: When I was a child, I remember my father would tell me the story of a young Baptist minister who had gone North to seek his fame and fortune. After he had become very successful, the pastor of his former small Southern church extended an invitation to return home for a visit and preach before his old congregation. Well, this minister could hardly refuse such an offer; in fact, he was rather proud at the thought of coming back and showin' the folk how successful he had become. He decided to bring his seven-year-old son with him, to teach him a lesson about his history . . . his roots. When the minister returned to his old church he was moved so much

THE MEETING 153

that he proceeded to give one of the best sermons of his life . . . had the congregation rollin' from one emotion to another. When it was all over the pastor threw his arms around the young minister and said: "John, that was a truly moving and inspirational sermon . . . I wish we could give you some kind of honorarium, but as you know, our church is not doing so well."

[*Both* MALCOLM *and* DR. KING *laugh.*]

John just waved the pastor off and said that was fine; it was payment enough simply to return home for a visit. As John and his son were leaving, they passed the church collection box. John stopped and took out a crisp new ten dollar bill and placed it in the box. He and his son then proceeded out of the church to the parking lot. As they were getting into the car, all of a sudden the pastor came running outside calling John's name. As the pastor caught up to John he said: "I know you don't want any payment, but we just couldn't let you leave without at least a token of our appreciation." The pastor handed John a crisp new ten dollar bill which John immediately recognized as the one he had placed in the collection box just moments before. He took the money, exchanged final farewells with the pastor and got into his car. After a moment or two, he looked at his son, smiling proudly and confidently and said: "Son, I hope this teaches you a lesson." His son nodded, looked at his father and said: "Yes dad, it has. If you had given more, you would have gotten more."

[MALCOLM *laughs, but* DR. KING *smiles sadly. He gives a quiet and distant look, then softly to* MALCOLM *he says:*]

We all have to give more, Malcolm. More than we thought we needed to; sometimes more than we thought we had to give.
MALCOLM: We will both give our lives for this thing we call "freedom." You know that, don't you?
DR. KING: Yes. I know that.
MALCOLM: Is there anything we can do to change our history, Martin?
DR. KING: History is always more important than the men and events that make it. History had to bring us together, at least once, to see if we could change it.
MALCOLM: We *did* change it, didn't we, Reverend?

[*Pause.*]

It just didn't make a difference.
DR. KING: Neither one of us will be here to know that.
MALCOLM: No. I suspect not. Do you respect me, Martin?
DR. KING: I will always be against violence, Malcolm, regardless of the cause.

MALCOLM: [*Almost painfully.*] I asked you if you respected me, and you speak of violence. Is that all you see?
DR. KING: [*He moves slowly toward the window.*] You don't need to ask me that, Malcolm. Just walk out there on those streets. The eyes of the dead come alive in your presence. They believe in you, and because of that they are beginning to believe in themselves. You would have made one hell of a Baptist preacher!
MALCOLM: [*Smiles warmly.*] My father would have been pleased to know that.

[*Pause.*]

I suppose we will not be seeing much of each other?
DR. KING: No. I imagine we won't.
MALCOLM: Then I should be getting you back home. It's rather late.
DR. KING: Yes. It is.

[*Both men rise.* DR. KING *begins to put on his jacket, then coat.* MALCOLM *gives* DR. KING *his hat.*]

MALCOLM: Rashad will take you downstairs. My driver is waiting for you. He will take you where you need to go.
DR. KING: I appreciate that.

[*They walk toward the door.*]

MALCOLM: We could have made quite a team.
DR. KING: We *have* made quite a team. Most persons just didn't realize it.
MALCOLM: [*Smiles.*] May they be ignorant a little while longer.
DR. KING: Amen to that.
MALCOLM: Allah be praised.

[*Both men shake hands, then suddenly embrace, neither knowing who started it. After a moment or two, they look at each other in silence, an arm's length apart.*]

I never meant to hurt you with anything I might have said publicly. It's important to me that you know that.
DR. KING: It's important to me that you told me.
MALCOLM: Maybe, there was enough time after all.
DR. KING: For what?
MALCOLM: For friendship.
DR. KING: [*Smiles warmly.*] Take care of yourself, Malcolm.
MALCOLM: Goodbye, Martin.

[DR. KING *exits.* MALCOLM *looks at the door which is still partially open. He says softly:*]

Allah . . . protect the dreamer.

[MALCOLM *smiles warmly and then notices the doll. He picks it up and stares at it, sadly at first. Then he shakes his head and says:*]

And a child shall lead them.

[MALCOLM *chuckles, then laughs. He moves toward the window and looks out on his beloved Harlem. He studies the doll and begins to sing softly.*]

"YOU DON'T KNOW WHAT LOVE IS
UNTIL YOU'VE LEARNED THE MEANING OF THE BLUES
UNTIL YOU'VE LOVED A LOVE YOU'VE HAD TO LOSE
YOU DON'T KNOW WHAT LOVE IS"

[*He looks gently at the doll and whispers.*]

Let's go home.

[*The lights fade gently on him holding the doll. When the rest of the stage is dark the one light on* MALCOLM *fades quickly.*]

About Los Angeles Actors' Theatre/Los Angeles Theatre Center

The Los Angeles Actors' Theatre (LAAT) was founded in 1975, by the actor Ralph Waite, as a multicultural professional theatre producing original American plays and new interpretations of theatre classics.

The LAAT's Playwrights' Lab was started a year later by playwrights Patrick Tovatt, Miguel Piñero and then managing artist Bill Bushnell. By the summer of 1977 the first One-Act Festival was presented. This annual event expanded to include full-length plays and became the LAAT's *Festival of Premieres* in 1979. By 1983, the Festival gained a wide recognition and sustaining support from the Louis B. Mayer Foundation and the One-Act portion of the Festival was renamed the *Louis B. Mayer Playwrights' Festival.*

Since 1978, when Bill Bushnell became artistic producing director, the LAAT has presented over 200 world and West Coast premieres. Many of the plays originally produced at the LAAT have received additional productions nationally and internationally. Several LAAT productions, like *TWO BY SOUTH*, and the award-winning production of *WAITING FOR GODOT*, have been seen on national television, and their original production of *SECRET HONOR* has been made into a feature film by director Robert Altman.

In 1984, the prestigious Margo Jones Theater Award was presented to Bill Bushnell and the Los Angeles Actors' Theatre. And in the coming year of 1985, the LAAT will open its new Los Angeles Theatre Center which will be the cultural cornerstone in the revitilization of the entire historic Spring Street District in downtown Los Angeles. The new Theatre Center will house four legitimate theatres of varying sizes, restaurants and a bookstore.

As LAAT prepares to become the Los Angeles Theatre Center, it continues to sustain its purpose as the place where playwrights, actors, directors and designers can come together to create vital, entertaining, controversial, contemporary living theatre.

About the Playwrights

Craig Pettigrew began his professional career at the age of eighteen playing trumpet with the Rochester Philharmonic. After attending both the Eastman School of Music and Northwestern University, (where he earned his degree in Film Production), Craig gravitated to Los Angeles, where he put his filmmaking skills to use for Home Box Office and 20th Century Fox. He is currently ghost-writing a novel and writing a screenplay for Warner Brothers.

Jim Geoghan is a native New Yorker who spent nine years in niteclub comedy before moving to Los Angeles. His plays have been part of the LAAT Festival of Premieres for three consecutive years. Other plays have been produced at the Actors Alley and the Beverly Hills Playhouse. He has been commissioned twice by Louisville Actors' Theatre and also writes for film and television.

Willard Manus has published three novels, *The Fixers, Mott the Hoople* and *The Fighting Men* recently published by Panjandrum Books. He has also contributed articles and short stories to, *The Nation, Holiday, Quest, New Letters, Venture, New York Times, Washington Post, Chicago Tribune,* and *The Observer.* He has been publicity director of the Macmillan Company, and now reviews plays and films for *The Century City News* and *The Financial Post.*

Joseph Scott Kierland is a graduate of the University of Connecticut and the Yale Drama School. He has won twelve national and international awards for playwrighting, and has been Playwright-in-Residence at the Lincoln Center for the Performing Arts, the Lab Theatre and Brandeis University. He is presently a Playwright-in-Residence at the LAAT and has been Director of the LAAT's Playwrights' Lab since 1980. Most recently, Mr. Kierland has written the film *O'HARA'S WIFE* and has four screenplays in production.

Kitty Johnson is a recipient of a 1983–84 playwrighting grant from the National Endowment for the Arts and is a Playwright-in-Residence at the Los Angeles Actors' Theatre. She was born and raised in Cincinnati, Ohio, and received a B.A. in English (dramatic literature) from Wilmington College.

About the Playwrights

Alan Ormsby is a screenwriter and playwright. His screenplays include *MY BODYGUARD*, *THE CAT PEOPLE*, and the forthcoming *TOUCH AND GO*, with Michael Keaton. Recipient of a Shubert Playwrighting Fellowship, his play *MOMSIE AND THE MIDNIGHT BRIDE* was performed at the Mark Taper Forum in the *New Theatre For Now* series. Subsequently, *THEY WON'T LET ME PAY YOUR RENT, JACK!* was performed at the Los Angeles Actors' Theatre as part of their annual Festival.

Paul Minx's *PROWLERS* won a Drama-Logue Award for Playwriting when it was first produced at LAAT in 1980. It was subsequently seen at the Yale Cabaret, Missouri Repertory Theatre and the University of Iowa. Two other plays, *BLOOD ENGINE* and *SHOOT OUT THE LIGHTS* have also been produced at LAAT. *HOME REMEDIES* was a selection at the Eugene O'Neill National Playwrights' Conference in 1981, and was produced the next year in New York at the Actors' Outlet. Mr. Minx was educated at the University of Iowa Writers' Workshop and the Yale School of Drama and now lives in New York City.

Jeff Stetson is currently a University Dean for the California State University system. He completed his doctoral at Boston University and has been awarded the Whitney Young Jr. Fellowship at Boston University, and the Outstanding Black Educator Award for 1977. Several of Mr. Stetson's poems have also been featured in the recent production, *Romance: An Evening of Poetry and Jazz* at the Chandler Pavilion in Los Angeles.

About the Producers

Adam Leipzig has worked on the *Louis B. Mayer Playwrights' Festival* since 1979, and has been its co-producer since 1980. As Dramaturg, he coordinates the programming of plays, music, dance, intermedia/performance and poetry for the Los Angeles Theatre Center.

Diane White is a recipient of the Los Angeles Drama Critics Circle's Margaret Harford Award for distinguished achievement in theatre, which specifically cited her productions of LAAT's *Festival of Premieres* and the *Louis B. Mayer Playwrights' Festival*. She has been with LAAT since its inception in 1975.

Other Books of Interest From Panjandrum*

FOUR TEXTS by Antonin Artaud (Translated by Clayton Eshleman and Norman Glass). ($6.95 pap., $15.95 cl.) 130 pp.
Four of the most impressive texts that Artaud completed at the height and end of his career. Included are two of his letter-essays, his famous statement on Nerval and a summation piece on his relationship to Surrealism addressed to Brêton; Artaud's poetic masterpiece, *"Artaud le Mômo"*; and the final major work of his life, *"Pour en finir avec le jugement de dieu"* ("To have done with the judgement of God").

MIMES ON MIMING: WRITINGS ON THE ART OF MIME edited by Bari Rolfe. ($6.95 pap., $15.95 cl.) 256 pp.
This scholarly yet entertaining work, using the performers' own words, begins with mime in ancient Greece and Rome and brings us to the present with 68 entries, including Marceau, Chaplin, Keaton, Lecoq, Shields, Goslar, Enters, Barrault, Van Dyke and even Woody Allen.

THE MENUHINS: A FAMILY ODYSSEY by Lionel Menuhin Rolfe. ($12.95 cl.) 256 pp.
The first biography of the musical Menuhin prodigies, including the great violinist Yehudi and his celebrated sisters, Yaltah and Hephzibah. "A wholly engrossing, sincerely wrought document of positive Jewish interest."—*B'nai Brith Messenger*.

ALFRED JARRY: THE MAN WITH THE AXE by Nigey Lennon. ($6.95 pap., $15.95 cl.) 136 pp. (Illus. by Bill Griffith.)
The first English-language biography of Jarry, author of *Ubu Roi*, which ushered in the era of Theatre of the Absurd, Surrealism, Nihilism, and Dadaism.

SEA URCHIN HARAKIRI: SELECTED POEMS by Bernard Bador (Trans. by Clayton Eshleman). ($6.95 pap., $15.95 cl.) 130 pp. *Forthcoming*.
"What makes these poems unique is the way in which they utilize various Surrealist strategies (especially black humor, Objective Hazard, and the estrangement of sensation) without edging in under the canopy of an established Surrealist voice."—From the Introduction by C. Eshleman. With an afterword by Robert Kelly. A bi-lingual edition.

TOUT A COUP: 32 POEMS BY VICENTE HUIDOBRO (Trans. by Geoffrey Young). ($5.95 pp., $10.95 cl.) 80 pp. *Forthcoming*.

TRES INMENSAS NOVELAS WITH TRES NOVELAS EJEMPLARES (Three Immense Novels with Three Exemplary Novels) by V. Huidobro and Hans Arp (Trans. by Tom Raworth). ($6.95 pap., $15.95 cl.) 150 pp. *Forthcoming*.
First English translation of this experimental, Surrealist collaboration first published in Spanish in 1931.

*This is a partial list; free catalogue on request.